LATIN AMERICA
A BROADER WORLD ROLE

LATIN AMERICA

A BROADER WORLD ROLE

By

ADALBERT KRIEGER VASENA

&

JAVIER PAZOS

ERNEST BENN LIMITED / LONDON AND TONBRIDGE

TOTOWA / NEW JERSEY / ROWMAN AND LITTLEFIELD

First published *1973* by *Ernest Benn Limited*
Sovereign Way, Tonbridge, Kent &
25 New Street Square, Fleet Street, London, EC4A 3JA

and in the USA 1973 by Rowman and Littlefield

Distributed in Canada by
The General Publishing Company Limited, Toronto

© *The Atlantic Institute 1973*

ISBN 0 510-27402-1

ISBN 0-87471-424-9 (USA)

Printed in Great Britain

Preface

THIS BOOK WAS written by Adalbert Krieger Vasena and Javier Pazos under the auspices of the Atlantic Institute for International Affairs. The Institute wishes to acknowledge the financial and other collaboration of the Organization of American States (OAS), the Inter-American Development Bank (IDB), and the Adela Investment Company. The financial contributions of the OAS, the IDB, and Adela in no way signify responsibility for any proposals or recommendations made in the book, nor indeed for any of the contents.

In addition to these sponsoring organizations, the work has had the benefit of the support of several prominent European private entities. The Tinker Foundation also assisted the study and financed the meeting of Young Leaders from Latin America, North America, Japan and Europe that was held in Mexico City in May 1972.

During the preparation of this book, an international Steering Committee, chaired by Mr Víctor Urquidi, President of the Colegio de México, advised on the project. The other members of the Committee – besides the authors and the chairman – were Dr Herman Abs (Germany), Dr Francis Bregha (Canada), Dr Rubens Costa (Brazil), Dr Lincoln Gordon (United States), Dr Aurelio Peccei (Italy), Sir Geoffrey Wallinger (Britain), and Mr John Tuthill and Professor Pierre Uri of the Atlantic Institute for International Affairs.

The authors were assisted by Mr Gerald Olsen, who also served as the executive officer of the Steering Committee. Joan Pearce, Librarian at the Atlantic Institute for International Affairs, undertook the difficult task of translating from Spanish to English and, together with David Huelin of Lloyds & Bolsa International Bank, edited the final version. The authors also drew on papers prepared for the project by Francis Bregha, Akio Hosono, David Huelin, Esteban Ivovich, Elba Kybal, Santiago Macario, and Eloy Mestre. The staff of the Atlantic Institute for International Affairs made

great efforts to ensure that the various drafts were completed on time.

The sole responsibility for the opinions expressed in this book rests with the joint authors, though the members of the Steering Committee have in a personal capacity indicated their concurrence with the general themes expressed. On some major points, members of the Steering Committee have wished to elaborate further or to record a differing view. These comments are published as an appendix. In his contribution Víctor Urquidi dissents from parts of the authors' interpretation and analysis of Latin America's development problems. The domestic aspects of these views are shared by Lincoln Gordon, who himself stresses the need for a more active United States policy towards the region. Dr Gordon also endorses the comments of Aurelio Peccei, which deal with the broad context of international economic relations, particularly some important non-economic factors that impinge on it, that Latin America will need to consider. Pierre Uri presents a summary of his forthcoming book, *Development without Dependence*, which goes beyond the problems of the Latin American continent, and suggests indirect means of dealing with the issues of development rather than with the governments of the developing countries. Lastly, the role of the private sector is discussed by Sir Geoffrey Wallinger. For my part, I would like to associate myself with the comments made by Dr Gordon on the population problem, and with the general themes outlined by Mr Urquidi and Dr Peccei.

The chief objective of this study is to throw light on certain major – and frequently disturbing – trends associated with Latin America's relationship with the industrialized world. The authors and the Steering Committee are convinced that in North America, Europe, and Japan, far too little attention is being given to Latin America; they have therefore sought to present these issues in a provocative manner. The authors do not seek easy acceptance; they do seek a dialogue that will attract the attention of men of goodwill to problems that have too long remained unsolved and have impeded Latin America's development.

Latin America comprises various types of states, with widely different resources and in diverse stages of development. It is not possible to generalize in terms of 'Latin American' industrial or agricultural development, growth, inflation, foreign trade, or the like. But one thing is clearly common to the entire area: its citizens are becoming increasingly aware that they are not getting a fair share of what the world has to offer.

To recognize a maldistribution of the good things of life is one thing; to correct it is another. Neither the authors of this book nor the members of the Steering Committee claim that it deals with every issue. They do, however, believe they have defined at least some of the most pressing current problems and have pointed the way towards possible solutions. If sometimes these definitions seem to be too crudely sketched, it is hoped the reader will bear in mind the authors' determination sharply to call attention to issues that have for too long been treated with silence or with anodyne pronouncements.

This tendency on the part of many Latin Americans, Europeans, North Americans, and Japanese to evade problems and seek palliatives is regrettable. The authors have attempted to stimulate serious thought on these matters; whatever dissent there may be, they trust it will be clear – and public. At least, the debate will have begun.

Paris
April 1973

JOHN W. TUTHILL
Director General

Introductory Note

THE ATLANTIC INSTITUTE has given us the opportunity of looking at Latin America from an angle very different from the one we are used to within the region, where we are involved in day-to-day problems. The picture is not rosy; on the contrary, it is disquieting. One sees with anxiety the contrast between Latin America's immense potential and its declining significance in the world economy. The only explanation one dare venture is that Latin America has set its sights too low in the post-war period. If this book is a contribution to raising these sights, so that Latin America endeavours to participate more fully in the world economy and to achieve the development that its citizens deserve, we shall have accomplished our task.

Paris,
April 1973

A.K.V.
J.P.

Contents

PART ONE

Past and Potential

Chapter 1

Latin America in a Changing World

THE EARLY 1970s find Latin America at an intermediate stage of development. The region's semi-development presents many of the problems of both the developing and the industrialized countries, but it also offers unique opportunities; the Latin American countries' capacity for growth is much larger than that of most other developing regions, and they enjoy the advantage of being able to avoid many of the economic and social mistakes committed by the industrialized countries. The region is capable of achieving very rapid growth and of establishing a successful development pattern peculiar to Latin America, which could embrace the best and discard the worst aspects of the experience of the industrialized countries. This is the goal that Latin America should set itself but, judged by such a standard, the present state of affairs is disappointing. The region's history and potential are not such as to justify its recent shortcomings, least of all the fact that since the Second World War Latin America's importance in the world has gradually dwindled.

A hundred years ago Latin America was at little or no disadvantage in relation to many of the countries that now compose the industrialized world. The Latin American countries had been independent republics for 50 years at a time when Italy had only just become a nation state, and the United States was still recovering from the disruptions of the Civil War. In 1870 the agricultural sector in Latin America was thriving, whereas the Austro-Hungarian Empire was still adjusting itself to the abolition of the feudal system. Extensive railway systems were being built in the larger Latin American countries, while 20 more years were to pass before Russia began work on the Trans-Siberian Railway. In certain commodities several Latin American countries were already established as major trade partners of western Europe at a time when in Japan the restored Meiji dynasty had just taken the first step towards modernization by opening the country's ports to foreign trade. Africa and Asia, except for India, were scarcely beginning to emerge on the international scene. Western Europe treated most Far Eastern countries, including China, as mere trading posts, and had colonized less than one-tenth of Africa. Argentina and Mexico were each exporting more than the entire continent of Africa, excluding South Africa.

Latin America enjoyed an economic status approaching that of the 'old dominions' of the British Empire, with which it shared a number of common antecedents. Canada and Australia, for example, had also been colonized by European powers, and for many years their external economic relations had been restricted to a mercantile system, in which their role was to supply raw materials and foodstuffs to the metropolitan nations. The boom in world trade in the late nineteenth and early twentieth centuries enabled Canada and Australia, like Latin America, to expand their export sectors, largely in primary products, and also to begin to industrialize. In the 1930s, the level of development of Canada and Australia was comparable with that of some Latin American countries, such as Argentina, Brazil, and Mexico.

Argentina, Australia, and Canada had similar export earnings until the beginning of the post-war period, but Canada and Australia then drew rapidly ahead. Today the *per capita* income of Canada is three times that of Argentina, and Australia's *per capita* income is four times that of Mexico. Canada, an original member of the Group of Ten, is now a creditor country in the Inter-American Development Bank, and Australia has recently joined the OECD. Latin America, on the other hand, is usually classed as part of the developing world, is in general a debtor region, and at present exerts relatively little influence in world economic affairs.

The slow pace of Latin America's advance is explained to a very large extent by the region's failure during the past 25 years to face straightforwardly the cardinal problem of its development strategy: that of improving and expanding its agricultural and industrial productive capacity in order both to furnish internal needs and to generate autonomously the external resources essential to independent and continued development.

The post-war period has witnessed progress: economic growth rates have on the whole been quite high, education and health services have improved substantially, much investment has gone into infrastructure, real wages have generally increased, and a higher proportion of income has accrued to the middle social groups. The process of economic and social development has not, however, gathered sufficient momentum for Latin America to pass beyond a state that may be described as one of semi-development. Not surprisingly, the many problems associated with that state, such as unemployment, uneven income distribution, rapid population growth, inflation, and balance-of-payments difficulties, have assumed increasing importance. As a result, the priorities of development strategies have been blurred; attempts to solve problems that are merely symptoms of semi-development have been unsuccessful because they have diverted energy and attention from the fundamental need : that of superseding semi-development itself, which can be met only by increasing productivity and efficiency.

Because Latin America has neglected to give priority to production within an overall development strategy, its participation in the world economy has steadily declined. The region's share of international trade has fallen alarmingly : from 11 per cent in 1950 to less than 5 per cent in 1972. The total exports of Latin America to markets outside the region amount to no more than those of Italy, whose circumstances in 1945 were no more propitious than those of many Latin American countries. Furthermore, whereas in 1950 almost 40 per cent of all United States foreign investment was in Latin America, by 1971 the proportion had fallen to a figure well below 15 per cent.

The reduction of Latin America's role in the international economy has been extremely damaging. It has created a progressive dependence on external borrowing because, to satisfy domestic social and economic expectations, Latin American governments have had to supplement inadequate export earnings with 'aid' from 'donor' countries. At the same time, it has reinforced the defeatist attitude that originated in the region during the Depression, to the point that most Latin Americans have become convinced that their future depends largely on outside forces. Besides creating dependence, both real and imagined, the diminution of Latin America's participation in the world economy has greatly decreased its bargaining power in international trade and finance. This is particularly serious at a moment when the framework of international economic relations is about to undergo reforms that will mould it for some years to come.

The collapse of world trade during the Depression and the difficulties that subsequently confronted exports of primary products forced the Latin Americans to devise inward-looking formulas for development. Far from leading to economic autonomy, this policy subsequently increased the dependence of the region on the industrialized countries, though not through any deliberate intention on their part. While Latin America has increasingly to rely on the industrialized countries for the fundamental elements of its development, such as technology, managerial know-how, and credit, the industrialized countries have been losing interest in the region. The remarkable technological advances of the post-war era have made the industrialized countries progressively less dependent on external sources of raw materials, because there are more and more possibilities of economically substituting one raw material for another. And Latin America, which has continued to act as a supplier of raw materials to the world market, has only quite recently – in many cases more loquaciously than effectively, and without going to the nub of the issue – started to be concerned about its productive inadequacy as a cause of its dependence.

Ironically, Latin Americans have devoted much time and energy to constructing an over-elaborate theory of 'dependence'. The analyses and conclusions of the early advocates of inward-looking development were for the most part valid, but they came to be distended out of all proportion. Notions such as the deterioration in the terms of trade, the competitive disadvantage of developing countries in the production of manufactures, the classification of countries into those of the centre and those constituting the periphery, and the political implications of capital movements and transfers of technology were combined to form an all-embracing theory.

In essence, the theory of dependence holds that the important economic decision-making centres do not lie in Latin America, either because of the mechanisms of international trade and finance or, more recently, because of the power of foreign-owned transnational corporations. Such a concept is conducive to inaction, since its logical conclusion is that there is little that Latin Americans can do to escape from dependence unless important changes in attitude occur among the industrialized countries. This is a naïve position that can only result in Latin America's losing yet more time before it is able to improve the conditions of its people by responding to their need for more goods and better services.

During the past decade, the tendency to procrastinate has been facilitated by large inflows of external financing, which have supplemented Latin America's inadequate export earnings. This situation is unlikely to last much longer. It was only because of political considerations that Latin America was able to establish the type of donor-recipient relationship conceived in the joint United States-Latin American programme of the Alliance for Progress. The Cold War, and after it the ideological struggle to which so-called peaceful co-existence gave rise, were waged world-wide. Latin America retained its importance as an area of confrontation to which the United States attached special significance because of historical ties and strategic factors.

There is now, however, a trend in international relations towards putting ideological considerations to one side. East-West tensions are giving way to a tacit global understanding between the United States and the Soviet Union on security issues. At the same time, with Britain's entry into the Economic Community, Europe is gaining political as well as economic importance; Japan's economic pre-eminence implies her resumption of a major political role in the world; and China is exchanging her isolated place as an ideological revolutionary vanguard for that of a power in world politics.

In economic as in political affairs, the bipolar world centred on the United States and the Soviet Union is rapidly becoming a multi-polar world. The Soviet Union and the other Comecon countries are improving their economic relations with the United States, western Europe, and Japan, while China is entering the world economic scene. The importance of these developments is enhanced by the possibility that the socialist countries may participate in future trade and monetary arrangements within the institutional framework established by the other industrialized countries.

Within the Western industrialized world too, much has changed in the past 25 years. The economic preponderance of the United States has declined, while commercial power has become more evenly balanced between Europe, Japan, and North America; this has brought about many changes in international financial relations, and the world's failure to adjust the machinery of the international monetary system to meet these new pressures led to the series of crises that began in 1971.

International economic relations are undergoing a broad revision. The economic power of the most advanced countries, and the direction and composition of world trade, are very different from those on which the Bretton Woods monetary system was constructed on the basis of the gold-dollar standard. A realignment of economic and political power centres is already becoming apparent. For some time, each of the industrialized countries will be preoccupied with ensuring for itself a favourable position in the new balance of power. Many of them also face serious internal economic problems that will consume much of their attention and may accentuate their inward-looking stance. It seems likely that the coming years will see the relations between the industrialized and the developing countries being influenced progressively less by political considerations and more by purely economic interest.

These trends are likely to frustrate the developing countries' hopes of negotiating better terms for themselves within the world economy. These hopes are in any case largely based on the false assumptions that there is a clear-cut distinction between developed and developing countries, and that the latter have many interests in common. The meeting of UNCTAD III in April and May 1972 demonstrated how mistaken was the belief that 100 countries, with divergent interests, could mount an effective position from which to negotiate with the tightly knit group of a few powerful industrial countries, in the complexities of international economic relations.

Though the current process of realignment dims the prospects of the developing countries, as a group, for procuring a fairer deal in the world economy, it offers an opportunity for Latin America to resume a more important role. On certain issues, Latin America has good reason to identify itself with the developing world in any substantive negotiations with the industrialized countries. Such a case would be the linking of international development finance to the system of international liquidity based on Special Drawing Rights. What Latin America should avoid is the submerging of its existing relations with the industrialized world in a fruitless confrontation between the developing and the developed countries. The Latin American countries as a group have reached a stage of semi-development, which places them in a better position than the less developed countries to benefit from the present fluid state of international economic relations by negotiating better export opportunities and financial arrangements with the developed nations.

Latin America appears, however, to be slow in perceiving the radical shift that has taken place, though the region is already feeling its repercussions. Discussions in Latin American forums are an echo of the past, in the forms both of documented statements about the need for external financing and of attacks by the 'theorists of dependence' on a colonialism that is in fact less and less interested in colonizing. This attitude, which is manifested by Latin Americans throughout the ideological spectrum, emanates from an exaggerated notion of the area's importance and of the industrialized countries' interest in it, and implies that Latin America possesses great bargaining power in international negotiations.

In fact, if the region is to acquire adequate international bargaining power for it to defend its interests effectively and enter into a constructive relationship with the industrialized countries, the Latin American countries must adopt more pragmatic attitudes than in the past. They must concentrate their efforts on developing competitive lines of production that will rapidly increase their share of world trade. This alone, however, is not enough; realistic formulas must be found for promoting a rapid increase in trade within the region and a greater degree of economic integration. This is indispensable if Latin America is to achieve the unity necessary for asserting greater international bargaining power. Some of the larger countries may think themselves important enough not to need to reckon with their smaller neighbours, but the shallowness of this attitude is evident if any individual country's significance in the world economy is compared with the position that the region as a whole could acquire. Indeed, the Latin American countries acting together could claim a new international standing for the region, whereas if they continue to act separately, they will find themselves left on the sidelines.

Integration is only a first step, however, in the expansion of the region's world role. Latin America needs to extend its role beyond the confines of the inter-American system. The United States will of course continue to be of great importance to the region, particularly as a growing market for its exports of both primary and manufactured products, and as a source of capital and technology; but it is already recognized that this partnership by itself is insufficient. Latin America should set about strengthening its economic links with western Europe, Japan, the socialist countries, Canada, and Australia. To foster a new and constructive relationship with the developed world, Latin America will not only need clearly defined and competently implemented development strategies and a flourishing regional trade, but will also have to set up the appropriate institutional machinery for dealing with the industrialized countries.

Chapter 2

The Role of Latin America in the International Economy

I. THE INTERNATIONAL DIVISION OF LABOUR BEFORE THE FIRST WORLD WAR

DURING THE EIGHTEENTH CENTURY, the restrictive mercantilist measures imposed by Spain and Portugal on their colonies became increasingly onerous as the Spanish and Portuguese economies continued to stagnate, and as the Latin American ruling classes increasingly aspired to a more active role in international trade. The Napoleonic occupation of the Iberian Peninsula in the early years of the nineteenth century provided the colonies with the opportunity to loosen their ties with the metropolis, and subsequently to win their independence. After achieving independence the Latin American countries established major economic links with European countries, particularly with Britain. These were rapidly expanded as the economic and demographic growth that accompanied the industrial revolution created a rising demand in Europe for foodstuffs and raw materials, and as the introduction of more advanced means of transport, beginning with steel steamships and later the development of refrigeration, enabled this demand to be satisfied from abroad.

Britain took advantage of her lead in the industrial revolution to institute a system of free trade with countries whose economies were complementary to her own. Though the system began to weaken after the 1870s, it continued, until the First World War, to enable Latin America to participate in the international division of labour as an exporter of raw materials and an importer of manufactured goods and capital, both physical and financial. The rise in exports, which was spectacular in such cases as nitrates from Chile, guano from Peru, sugar from Cuba, and cattle and cereals from Argentina, brought about rapid economic growth in various parts of Latin America.

At the end of the last century Latin America's share of world trade was not very much less than that of the United States. By 1890 the region's share of world exports had reached 8 per cent or probably higher,[1] and the level was maintained at about 10 per cent during the first three decades of the twentieth century. The value of exports almost trebled between 1890 and the beginning of the First World War, and then doubled between 1913 and the beginning of the Depression of the 1930s.

Latin America's importance in the international economy can also be appreciated from the amount of investment it attracted from Britain, who before the First World War was the world's principal supplier of capital. By 1913, the investment placed by Britain in the region exceeded that in India or the United States, and was second only to British investment in the 'old dominions' – that is, Canada, Australia, and New Zealand – together.

Distribution of British Foreign Investment 1870 and 1913
(percentages)

	1870	*1913*
Dominions	12	30
India	21	10.5
Africa (ex South Africa)	—	2.5
TOTAL BRITISH EMPIRE	36	46
Europe	25	6
Latin America	10.5	22
United States	27	19
Others	3.5	7
WORLD TOTAL	100	100

Source: Michael Barratt Brown, *After Imperialism* (London: Heinemann, 1963), p. 110.

There were also sizeable French and German investments in Latin America, as well as from other European countries. On the eve of the First World War total European investment in Latin America amounted to $6,800 million at 1914 values.[2] This European capital, and from the turn of the century United States capital too, flowed into Latin America to develop the production and exports of raw materials, at the same time financing the necessary infrastructure. Foreign capital brought with it technologically advanced production that not only benefited those enterprises in which foreign capital was directly involved, but also significantly affected the rest of the economy. During the period 1875–1913, foreign investment facilitated a big increase in Latin America's trade and the creation of a generally substantial favourable trade balance. In contrast to what has happened since the Second World War, the foreign exchange resources needed to repay the dividends on foreign investment were provided by export earnings generated by the investment itself.

Allied with the growth in foreign trade and investment were a process of social modernization, the extension of education, and the expansion of domestic production, including industrial production. In Mexico real *per capita* domestic product increased at an average annual rate of 3.1 per cent between 1900 and 1910. In Brazil the railway network expanded from 3,400 to 21,300 kilometres between 1880 and 1910, and between then and the beginning of the First World War coffee exports more than quadrupled. In Argentina the population doubled between 1890 and 1914, while cereal exports increased fivefold and exports of refrigerated meat rose from 27,000 metric tons to 376,000 tons.

Contacts between Latin America and Europe in the last decades of the nineteenth and first decades of the twentieth centuries included immigration from most of the countries of Europe, especially from Spain, Portugal, and Italy, countries with which Latin America had only tenuous commercial and financial links but major cultural ties. The first decade of the twentieth century witnessed the peak of Latin America's economic relations with Europe. Sixty-five per cent of the region's export trade was towards the Old Continent, and of all investments in Latin America at the start of the First World War some three-quarters were of European origin. After 1914 European investment and trade with Latin America began to diminish while economic relations with the United States, which had got under way in the second half of the nineteenth century, began to expand more rapidly.

II. GROWING UNITED STATES INVOLVEMENT

By the end of the First World War, Latin America's economic relations with the United States were assuming greater importance than its relations with Europe, as much in trade as in finance. As a developing country, during the nineteenth century, the United States had been an importer of capital. Towards the end of the century, however, industrial expansion led to a growing interest in external markets and in supplies of minerals and tropical products. United States trade with Latin America increased and direct investment began to flow, especially to the Caribbean countries, Mexico, and Central America. Whereas in 1897 the sum of United States investment in Latin America was only about $300 million, two-thirds of which was in Mexico, at the end of the First World War it had risen to $2,400 million, and by 1929 it represented more than 40 per cent of the total foreign investment in Latin America.[3]

The Depression of the 1930s interrupted the flow of foreign investment. During the Second World War, German investments were expropriated, and after the war many British and French investments, especially in railways and public service companies, were nationalized with the reserves accumulated by unrequited exports during the war. The prostration of the European and Japanese economies after the war meant for Latin America that the United States was virtually the only exporter of capital in the Western world. United States foreign investment had already been resumed during the war, and in the post-war period by far exceeded all other direct and portfolio investment in the region.

The same trend appeared in Latin America's commercial relations. The First World War brought about a substantial decrease in the region's trade with Europe, and the United States soon became Latin America's principal trading partner. By 1938 imports from the United States represented about 40 per cent of total Latin American imports, and by the end of the Second World War, the United States accounted for more than half the region's external trade.

It was this growing commercial, as well as political, interest in Latin America that prompted the United States to propose a Pan-American conference, which was held in Washington in 1889; a permanent Pan-American organization, the International Union of American Republics, was subsequently established in Washington in 1890. For a time, after the First World War, the United States' chief concern in the Pan-American conferences was with commercial questions, and little sympathetic response was shown to Latin America's attempts to obtain understandings on non-intervention. A new era of inter-American relations was introduced by President Franklin Roosevelt at the Seventh Conference in Montevideo in 1933. Then, and again in 1937, the long sought-after non-intervention principle was accepted by the United States. Under Roosevelt's 'Good Neighbor Policy' progress was also made in economic co-operation. Reciprocal trade agreements with the United States were signed by some Latin American countries, and credits were granted through the Export-Import Bank.

After the war, the institutional framework of the inter-American system was strengthened by a reorganization that was recommended at the Chapultepec Conference in 1945, and culminated three years later in the drawing-up of the Charter of the Organization of American States. Economic co-operation was revived soon afterwards through President Truman's 'Point Four' aid programme, which provided technical as well as financial assistance, and in 1958, as a consequence of Latin American pressure, the United States accepted the need for an Inter-American Development Bank to make loans for economic and social development projects; this had been an objective of Latin American policy-makers for over a decade.

III. THE POST-WAR PERIOD : LESS TRADE AND DEEPER DEBT

The most outstanding characteristic of Latin America's international economic relations in the past quarter of a century is the constant shrinking of its share of world trade. Before and immediately after the Second World War, the region's share of world export trade was about 10 per cent, but this has fallen steadily, until in 1972 exports originating in Latin America represented less than 5 per cent of world exports. Had the region maintained the share that it had at the beginning of the 1950s, Latin American exports would today be worth more than $30,000 million, whereas in fact the value of its exports in 1972 was only about $16,000 million.

The slow growth of Latin America's exports has been accompanied by a change in the nature and purposes of private foreign investment and an increase, particularly after 1956, in public-sector external financing, generally classified as 'aid'; this has replaced the bond issues on the international financial markets that had commonly been made by Latin American public sector agencies before 1930, and also supplemented both portfolio and direct investment from abroad. Thus Latin America's relationship to the world economy in the post-war period has been quite different from what it was before the Depression, when Latin America was participating fully in the international division of labour of the time, and had an appropriate status as a borrower on the world's capital markets.

The expansion of international trade in the post-war world economy has been predominantly in manufactured goods. Industries in which productivity was low by the post-war standards of the United States were encouraged in Japan and Europe, where conditions were then more appropriate for labour-intensive activities. The United States was not the only country to stimulate trade in this manner, however; Sweden, for example, with the aim of exporting high productivity goods, ran down her relatively less productive textile industry and imported textiles. The international economy is thus being realigned in accordance with the principle of comparative advantage, this time on the basis of acquired technological skills and the achievement of high productivity rather than of endowments of natural resources.

With few exceptions, Latin America has not taken part in this realignment, but has continued to export mainly primary commodities. As a result, the region has suffered a substantial reduction in its share of international trade; this has occurred not in any specific market among the industrialized countries, but is general, the region's share having decreased in the United States' market as well as in those of Europe, Japan, and Canada. For similar reasons, the region's trade with other developing countries and with the socialist countries has remained minimal.

Latin America: Share in Total Value of Imports of Selected Regions
(percentages)

	1950	1960	1965	1970	1972
United States	35.4	21.3	17.3	11.9	10.0
Western Europe	8.5	6.0	5.1	3.8	3.2
Japan	9.0	6.4	8.1	6.5	5.3
Canada	4.3	5.4	4.7	3.9	3.3

Sources: United Nations, *Yearbook of International Trade Statistics* (for 1950); International Monetary Fund, *Direction of Trade* (for other years).

At the same time, there have been changes in the direction of Latin American exports, especially over the past decade. In the early 1950s, the United States was receiving almost 60 per cent of the value of Latin American exports to industrialized countries; by the end of the 1960s the proportion had dropped to 42 per cent, though the United States was still the region's biggest customer.[4] These changes do not reflect any conscious commercial policy on the part of Latin America, but rather the manner in which world trade was expanding.

Similar changes are occurring in Latin America's financial relations. By far the largest part (over 60 per cent) of foreign private investment still comes from the United States, but this share is gradually being reduced as European and Japanese direct investment moves into the region at a much brisker pace. Latin

Distribution of Latin American Exports to Industrialized Countries
(percentages)

	1938	1950	1960	1965	1970
United States	38.6	60.0	54.1	46.7	42.2
Canada	1.5	2.0	2.0	4.6	4.5
EEC	32.5	17.0	24.1	28.3	30.8
Britain	21.3	13.0	12.0	8.9	6.4
Other EFTA	4.1	5.0	4.6	5.9	6.8
Japan	2.0	3.0	3.2	5.6	9.3

Sources: United Nations, *Statistical Yearbook 1960* (for 1938 and 1950); IMF, *Direction of Trade* (for other years).

America's heavy protection of industry during the past 25 years has encouraged investment in the manufacturing sector, which now accounts for more than 40 per cent of the total, compared with 7 per cent in 1914. From the second half of the 1950s, foreign private investment in Latin America began to be supplemented to an increasing extent by private and public external loans, as well as by suppliers' credits, which enabled Latin America to acquire a larger volume of capital goods and industrial materials than would have been possible – given the slow growth of Latin American exports – without greatly increasing current account deficits. After 1961 many of these bilateral public sector financial flows from the United States, broadly classified as 'aid', were channelled through the programme of the Alliance for Progress.

The sums involved are not particularly large compared with the amount of foreign investment and external financing that was directed towards Latin America at the end of the last and the beginning of this century. To illustrate this point, it has been estimated that in 1914 the total value of foreign investment in the region was approximately $8,500 million.[5] This global figure, representing the nominal value of direct foreign investment in the region, plus bonds placed on world capital markets, was very large for the period and at 1970 values it can be equated, tentatively, to some $25,000 million. The current foreign contribution to Latin America's finance is estimated at $40,000 million and is obtained by adding the book value of all direct foreign investment in Latin America to the total foreign debt accumulated by the region up to 1969. The foreign capital per head of population was about twice as large in 1914 as in 1969.

The total capital inflow to Latin America in the past 25 years has not been very much larger than the financial resources received before the Second World War, but at that time exports were growing sufficiently fast to enable the region to meet all its obligations in debt servicing, profit remittances, and capital repatriations. In the past decade this has no longer been the case because exports have not grown rapidly enough for servicing and other payments to be provided out of current export income; Latin America has thus incurred a heavy debt burden, the servicing of which places an excessive strain on the region's limited foreign exchange earnings, and in general seems likely to increase for some years to come.

Public and officially guaranteed medium- and long-term external indebtedness rose from about $7,000 million in 1960 to over $20,000 million in 1972, with a yearly servicing of interest and amortization that now amounts to over $2,500 million. This servicing plus the remittance of profits on foreign investment and other private sector payments have come to represent yearly over 30 per cent of Latin American earnings from exports of goods and services. This high proportion can be attributed only in part to severe conditions of suppliers' credits, the low grant element in 'aid' to Latin America, or the sometimes excessive profits of foreign private investment. More basic than these widely canvassed explanations is the inadequacy of Latin America's exports. Had the region's economies been growing rapidly they would have required more, not less, external financing, but they would have been earning the foreign exchange needed to service the debts incurred. Not only would Latin America have been selling in greater volume, but manufactured goods would have accounted for a larger proportion of its exports, and the labour content of exports would have been correspondingly higher.

The fact that more than 90 per cent of Latin America's exports are primary products means that the growth of exports is slow, and that the region's external sectors are profoundly affected by market trends, and by restrictions and discriminations in the industrialized world, as well as many inelasticities of demand, all of which factors militate against primary commodities. Fluctuations occur in the prices of tropical agricultural products, such as sugar and coffee, which reflect changes in supply, and in the prices of others, such as meat, grains, fruit, and vegetable oils, because many developed countries rely on imports only to supplement their domestic production, which is variable. The markets for certain other primary products, including many minerals, are controlled by a small number of buyers, who influence prices. The prices of primary products are also affected by cyclical fluctuations and changes in the industrial activity of the developed countries. Moreover, consumer demand and the prices received by producing

Latin America: Changes in the Price of Selected Export Products
(percentages)

Products	1965–66	1966–67	1967–68	1968–69	1969–70
Coffee (Brazil)	—8.7	—7.0	—1.2	7.4	30.4
Copper (London)	18.6	—26.2	9.8	18.5	9.0
Frozen beef (Argentina)	—9.7	—18.6	34.6	—9.9	22.9
Cotton (Mexico)	—0.4	10.0	—1.2	—10.3	3.4
Bananas (New York)	—2.8	2.9	—4.2	4.3	12.5
Corn (Argentina)	—1.2	—5.8	6.6	8.5	—11.1

Source: IMF, *International Financial Statistics.*

countries are sometimes affected by internal taxes in the importing countries, as for example on coffee in Germany.

These wide fluctuations in world prices of primary exports, rather than the debatable 'secular deterioration' in the terms of trade, constitute the main policy concern of primary exporters. It is only comparatively recently that concerted action by the exporting countries has begun to break down the bargaining power of the purchasing companies; the member nations of the Organization of Petroleum Exporting Countries (OPEC) have achieved an appreciably stronger position, and the world's major copper exporters are attempting a similar strategy.

Latin America could reduce its heavy reliance on primary exports if it could substantially increase its exports of manufactured goods, but as yet it has failed to do so. At the beginning of the 1970s the proportion of manufactures in total Latin American exports was still below 10 per cent, compared with almost 20 per cent for the developing countries as a whole, if a strict definition of manufactures is used.[6] This composition of Latin American exports is not peculiar to any particular market, but is a phenomenon common to all markets, except within Latin America, where the proportion of manufactures to total exports is much higher.

In recent years the export performance in manufactured goods among the Latin American countries has improved noticeably. However, except in Brazil, where great strides have been made in

*Exports of Manufactures from Latin America**

To:	$ million at current prices		Annual growth rate (%)	
	1960	*1969*	*1960–69*	*1965–69*
World	269	1080	16.7	18.7
Developed market economy countries	187	536	12.4	20.0
Socialist countries	4	24	22.0	32.1
Latin America	58	500	27.0	16.5

* Standard International Tariff Classification headings 5, 6, 7, and 8, excluding 68.

Source: UNCTAD, *Review of Trade in Manufactures of the Developing Countries, 1960–1970.* TD/111 (Geneva, 10 December 1971), p. 23.

promoting exports of manufactures, the absolute level remains low, despite the impressive percentage increases, and affords no grounds for complacency about the state of the region's trade.

IV. THE ORIGINS AND IDEOLOGY OF IMPORT SUBSTITUTION

From an early date Latin Americans have been aware of the problems associated with excessive dependence on the unstable export prices of primary products. At the end of the last century the protectionist tendencies that had been common in Europe since the 1870s began to emerge in Latin America. The experience of the massive and prolonged contraction of trade, that they, like the rest of the world, subsequently underwent during the Depression and the Second World War inclined the Latin American countries to seek inward-looking development strategies.

All the Latin American countries suffered from the Depression, some more severely than others. By about 1920 Mexico's industrial growth had recovered from the effects of the revolution, but between 1928 and 1932 the average product at constant prices fell by 16 per cent and export receipts by 42 per cent. In Chile, exports were reduced to a very small fraction of their former level, and in Brazil, imports through Santos, the port serving São Paulo, fell from 1,479 thousand contos in 1928 to 440 thousand in 1932. Lastly, even though they were somewhat more diversified, Argentina's exports decreased by more than 55 per cent between 1928 and the trough years of the 1930s, because of the high elasticity of income from meat, her principal export.[7]

This drastic reduction in export trade during the world crisis of the 1930s compelled most Latin American governments to adopt a varied range of defensive policies aimed at maintaining employment levels and preventing internal economic activity from deteriorating further. Governments increased public expenditure, issuing money to do so, and economies were closed to imports, through exchange controls, quantitative restrictions, or tariff increases.

These economic policies, whose common characteristic was a substantially increased protection of industry, were rational in the circumstances and greatly stimulated the production of manufactures. The process of 'import substitution' that they introduced was reinforced during the Second World War by the difficulty of obtaining supplies from the industrialized countries.

These years of 'enforced protection', which lasted until the beginning of the 1950s when normal conditions of supply were reestablished in world markets, stimulated the development of industries not only in the larger countries, which had already started to industrialize, but also in those countries where industry had not taken firm root before the Depression. This industrial growth made the Latin American countries more confident in their capacity, and changed their attitude to the problems of development. Among Latin American politicians and economists a development strategy based on import substitution aroused great enthusiasm, which later became unconditional support; this was reinforced by a reaction against economists in the developed countries who in the early 1950s, ignoring the incipient expansion of trade in manufactures, had used an oversimplified version of the theory of comparative advantage to assert that the region should specialize almost exclusively in exports of primary commodities.

This development model, which ensued from the very real problems posed by the Depression and the Second World War, has inspired throughout the region policies that have attempted to reproduce the conditions of 'enforced protection' of the years before 1950. It was imagined that this would bring still greater acceleration of industrial development, the attraction of which was now enhanced by the illusion that it would end the state of dependence on international markets inherent among producers of raw materials.

The basic appeal of import substitution lay perhaps in its simplicity and in the direct and immediate results that it yielded. It was aimed at enabling the demand for manufactured goods (formerly catered for by imports) to be met by domestic production. Local entrepreneurs were offered the protection necessary to induce them to install manufacturing plants. Foreign capital tended increasingly to move away from the sluggish external sector towards the profitable internal manufacturing sector, for which it provided much of the technology and managerial talent.

From the beginning of the century, excessive protection of industry had been opposed by agricultural interests, which objected to the increase in the prices of industrial products, and hence in their own production costs, and feared adverse consequences for their competitive position in world markets. Opposition had come also from political parties representing the working classes who claimed that the price increases were detrimental to the people.[8] However, the forces of economic nationalism and economic ideology came out in defence of protection and prevailed over those who resisted it in defence of particular interests or simply in the name of sound economic policy. The decline in the economic importance of producers of primary goods caused them to lose political strength, and workers in protected industries earning high wages neutralized the unfavourable reactions of other workers.

After the Second World War, protection was adopted as the intellectual fashion, and assumed a variety of forms, from quantitative restrictions through tariffs to exchange rate differentials. Protection has certainly been excessive when viewed in the light of policies followed by developed and developing countries alike. To take only nominal tariffs, it has been estimated that in the early 1960s the levels for manufactured goods stood at 11.5 per cent in the United States, 11 per cent in the European Community, 6.6 per cent in Sweden, 16.1 per cent in Japan, and 30 per cent in Taiwan, compared with 99 per cent in Brazil and 144 per cent in Argentina.[9]

More than a decade ago it began to be apparent that too much had been expected from policies of exaggerated protection. Industrial development was not continuing to accelerate as had been hoped, and the state of external trade was deteriorating. Latin American leaders should have sought an alternative development strategy that would have provided for swifter and more efficient industrialization under moderate levels of protection. Instead they have fostered a 'development ideology' that has been dangerously inclined towards placing the blame for deficiencies within the region on the state of international markets supposedly beyond Latin America's control.

NOTES

[1] Until some two decades ago, statistics of volume and value of Latin American exports were generally lower than reality. Recording formalities were minimal or non-existent and in many cases producing companies were not obliged to record the value of exports. The most extreme instance occurred in Chile where, for accounting reasons, nitrates did not appear in the export statistics for many years.

[2] Of this, $3,600 million came from Britain, $1,200 million from France, $1,000 million from Germany, and $1,000 million from other European countries. See United Nations Department of Economic and Social Affairs, *Foreign Capital in Latin America* (New York, 1955).

[3] See Cleona Lewis, *America's Stake in International Investments* (Washington D.C.: Brookings Institution, 1938), appendix D, pp. 575–607.

[4] The reduction of this share can be attributed in part to the suspension of United States trade with Cuba in 1961, but it was also caused by the sluggishness of Latin American exports to the United States market.

[5] This estimate was made in *Foreign Capital in Latin America* (United Nations Department of Economic and Social Affairs, New York, 1955). A lower estimate of $7,800 million was made in the ECLA publication *External Financing in Latin America* (New York, 1965).

[6] This definition excludes some Standard International Tariff Classification headings, which comprise semi-finished primary materials, such as copper, with a very small amount of value added. ECLA, on the other hand, includes all the SITC headings in its definition of exports of manufactured goods from Latin America, in which case manufactured goods amount to about 18 per cent of total exports for 1970.

[7] Nacional Financiera, *La Política Industrial en el Desarrollo Económico de México* (Mexico, 1971), p. 29. Osvaldo Sunkel, 'Change and Frustration in Chile' in Claudio Veliz, ed., *Obstacles to Change in Latin America* (London: Oxford University Press, 1965), p. 121. Warren Dean, *The Industrialization of Sao Paulo 1880–1945* (Austin: University of Texas Institute of Latin American Studies, Latin American Monograph No. 17, 1969), p. 193.

[8] It is interesting to record the opposition to protection voiced by the Socialist Party founded in Argentina by the influential politician Juan B. Justo. See also debates in the Argentinian Congress on the subject of customs tariffs and trade with Britain, 1920–30.

[9] Ian Little, Tibor Scitovsky, and Maurice Scott, *Industry and Trade in Some Developing Countries: a Comparative Study* (London: Oxford University Press, for the OECD, 1970), pp. 162–3.

Chapter 3

Semi-Development

LATIN AMERICA AS A whole has reached a level of development that places it in an intermediate position between the industrialized countries and the rest of the developing world. Economic expansion during the past quarter of a century has brought improvements in economic and social welfare. The growth of the gross national product in Latin America, at an annual cumulative rate of over 4 per cent, has been higher than that attained by the industrialized countries in the past century.[1] Even in recent years, the growth rate of the industrialized countries has been on average no higher than Latin America's, except for Japan and a few European countries, such as East and West Germany and Yugoslavia.

The development of commercial agriculture has increased the region's nutritional level; meat and protein consumption is relatively high in comparison with income; the improvement of health services has reduced infant mortality and increased life expectancy; communication media have expanded; illiteracy has been greatly reduced; water supplies have been made more generally available; and there has been a marked increase in electricity consumption.

By the criteria of less developed regions, these achievements are, in general, gratifying. In Latin America, however, the usual standard of comparison is the industrialized countries; this gives rise to high expectations of improvement, so that the development achieved has aroused more frustration than satisfaction. The political Left maintains the dogma, though seriously challenged by ten years of Cuban experience, that only revolutionary changes would release a much greater development potential. The Centre, which has been most often in power in the past 25 years, feels unsure of the path that it is following. The Right is discontented because growth has not proceeded fast enough to compensate for the social changes that imperil the *status quo*.

The causes of this dissatisfaction can be directly or indirectly traced to the inward-looking development strategies that most Latin American countries have followed. These strategies have

35

Latin America: Annual Growth Rates of Population, Gross Domestic Product and per Capita Gross Domestic Product for 1947–57 and 1960–69*

	1947–57			1960–69		
	Popula-tion percent increase	GDP percent increase	Per capita GDP percent increase	Popula-tion percent increase	GDP percent increase	Per capita GDP percent increase
Argentina	2.0	2.1	0.1	1.6	3.9	2.3
Bolivia	2.1	0.8	—1.2	2.3	5.3	3.0
Brazil	2.9	5.7	2.8	2.9	6.0	3.1
Chile	2.2	3.3	1.2	2.4	4.7	2.3
Colombia	2.7	4.5	1.9	3.4	4.9	1.5
Ecuador	3.0	5.9	2.9	3.4	4.6	1.2
Mexico	2.9	6.2	3.3	3.5	6.9	3.4
Paraguay	2.4	very low	negative	3.3	4.3	1.0
Peru	2.3	4.8	2.6	3.1	5.6	2.5
Uruguay	1.2	low	negative	1.3	1.1	—0.2
Venezuela	3.5	8.2	4.7	3.3	4.3	1.0

* The 1947 figure is an annual average for the years 1945–49, as is the 1957 figure for 1955–59. The figures for 1960 and 1969 are for single years only.

Sources: For 1947 and 1957, ECLA, *The Economic Development of Latin America in the Post War Period* (New York: United Nations, 1964).

For 1960 and 1969, ECLA, *Economic Survey of Latin America 1970* and *Tendencies and Structures of the Latin American Economy*, May 1971.

impeded the sound progress in development that was warranted by the economic growth rates achieved. In all probability, more outward-looking strategies would have enabled the poorer sectors of society to obtain more, better, and cheaper goods and services; would have avoided the present-day high degree of international financial indebtedness and dependence on aid; and would have given the region greater international bargaining power by assuring it a bigger share of international trade and a larger degree of economic integration and hence political unity. Above all, such policies would have resulted in still higher growth rates which would have raised the region as a whole beyond its present level of semi-development. Even though the accomplishments of the post-war period fall below what could reasonably have been expected, there has nevertheless been sufficient progress for Latin America to reach a point from which it could achieve a major breakthrough in development in the course of the coming decades.

I. LATIN AMERICA AND THE DEVELOPING WORLD

By the standard of any socio-economic welfare indicator, the stage of development attained by Latin America stands out from that of other developing regions. The average *per capita* income in Latin America, which exceeds $600 at current prices, is equivalent to one-third of the average income of a citizen of the industrialized countries, but represents a standard of living about three times as high as that of the other developing areas. Despite this, the standard of living in some less developed regions of the continent, such as the north-east of Brazil, Upper Peru, some Caribbean islands, and parts of Mexico and Central America, is possibly similar to that of the poorest countries of the world.

Even so, people are healthier and life expectancy is higher than elsewhere in the developing regions. The daily *per capita* net food consumption in almost all Latin American countries is over 2,200 calories, a level that is rarely reached by other developing countries. Medical facilities, whether measured by the number of doctors or the number of hospital beds, are much more generally available than in other developing regions. Levels of education are generally much lower elsewhere in the developing world than in Latin America. Almost everywhere in Latin America the proportion of school-age children receiving primary education is at least 70 per cent, whereas this is the maximum level attained by most other developing countries. Likewise, the number of students receiving higher education for every 100,000 of the population in the rest of the developing regions is less than 250, a figure that is exceeded by virtually all Latin American countries.

Latin America's level of development is not the only respect in which it more closely resembles European countries, such as Italy, Greece, and Spain, than the developing countries of Africa, Asia, or Oceania. In its cultural patterns, social behaviour, and economic structures as well, the region has much in common with the developed countries. These similarities can be traced to the region's history.

The conquest and colonization of Latin America firmly implanted a common Iberian culture in the region. The process was carried out under the strict control of the Spanish and Portuguese crowns, and was inspired by the Catholic faith. The settlers were drawn largely from the lower nobility and the gentry, and in the Spanish colonies exerted a high degree of administrative organization, learned in the course of expelling the Moors from Spain. The determination of the rulers of Spain and Portugal to prevent the establishment of a powerful New World aristocracy, together with the active interest of the Catholic Church, meant that, although the conquered subjects were compelled to adopt the language, religion, and customs of the settlers, they were treated as equals under the law. This, to a great extent, accounts for the satisfactory way in which ethnic fusion was accomplished in Latin America.

Much later, particularly at the end of the last century and the beginning of this, Latin America received large quantities of immigrants who were easily assimilated, even when they were not of Iberian origin; such was the case of Germans and Yugoslavs in Chile, Italians in Argentina, Brazil, and Uruguay, and Japanese in Brazil. Today racial problems in Latin America are insignificant compared with those in several African and Asian countries, or indeed in the United States. Civil strife has been very scant, except for the Mexican revolution, which was violent because of the latent agrarian problem, and there have been revolutions, such as those in Bolivia and Cuba, that have achieved radical change without major bloodshed.

Most African and Asian states lack both the internal cohesion of the Latin American countries and their affinity with the industrialized countries. Development problems in Africa and Asia are exacerbated by the presence of disparate ethnic and linguistic groups, and social attitudes determined by religious beliefs. Asian countries such as India, Bangladesh, or Sri Lanka also suffer from acute over-population and from the difficulty of adapting deep-rooted cultural traditions to the very different forms of socio-economic organization that emerged from the industrial revolution in Europe. In the African countries south of the Sahara, national integration is seriously hindered because national frontiers are based on political or administrative divisions made during the colonial period, which do not coincide with the territorial boundaries of tribal or ethnic groups; from this has resulted the inclusion in one nation of mutually hostile peoples and the division of cohesive ethnic groups into separate national territories.

The low level of national integration in Asia and Africa is reflected in the large sections of the populations that are not incorporated into market economies. In these regions economic development has emanated from European elements, which, although flourishing and influential, are no more than enclaves within the indigenous societies; in Latin America, on the other hand, the process of economic development began after colonization, and subsequently independence, had already established a high degree of national integration. The incorporation of a much larger proportion of the population into the market economies of Latin America is demonstrated by the percentage of wage-earners in the agricultural work force, which is much higher even in a country such as Peru than in, for instance, Ghana or Indonesia.[2]

The proportion of wage-earners in the non-agricultural work force is also high in Latin American countries compared with those

Proportion of Male Wage Earners to Total
Economically Active Population
(percentages)

	Agriculture	All Sectors
Argentina	50	72
Brazil	26	55
Mexico	49	62
Peru	31	49
Ghana	9	20
Indonesia	20	28
Liberia	9	22

Source: International Labour Office, *Yearbook of Labour Statistics 1972* (Geneva, 1972).

of Asia and Africa, but this is an indication of bigger economic units and systems of production based not on individual craftsmen marketing their own wares, but on modern industrial and commercial establishments.

To class Latin America as part of the developing world in general is misleading. Though Latin America does share some development problems with Africa and Asia, it has far more in common with the industrialized countries. That this is not generally recognized is, to a large extent, Latin America's own fault. The region could have established a more distinct and impressive identity in international economic relations if it had made greater strides towards economic integration.

II. THE PATH TO ECONOMIC INTEGRATION

The Latin Americans' common historical bonds, and a psychological need to belong to and identify themselves with a physical and cultural entity that transcends the nation, have made Latin America one of the more peaceful regions of the world.[3] Unlike that of Europe, the political map of Latin America has changed very little since the nations became independent early in the last century. The changes that have occurred, moreover, have mostly been achieved through arbitration, rather than invasion or annexation.[4]

With the exception of the War of the Triple Alliance (between Paraguay on one side and Argentina, Brazil, and Uruguay on the other) in the middle of the last century, and the Pacific War (between Chile, Peru, and Bolivia), conflicts between Latin American countries have been slight and have cost few lives compared with conflicts in the rest of the world, especially between the industrialized countries. Even the bloody Chaco War between Bolivia and Paraguay in 1935 caused no more than 200,000 casualties, whereas the First World War took a toll of lives equivalent to the present population of Venezuela, and the Second World War caused more than 50 million deaths, counting civilians and soldiers, which is equivalent to the population of Mexico.[5]

Though the Iberian settlers introduced a degree of political, social, and cultural uniformity that has made for much mutual understanding among the Latin American countries, the region has never been altogether homogeneous. Colonization itself took various forms. For example, in Mexico, where the Spanish administrative headquarters were established in the region most densely populated by the indigenous inhabitants, national integration was, from the beginning, much greater than in Peru, where the administration was centred in the coastal town of Lima, away from most of the indigenous population concentrated in the highlands.

The development patterns that emerged in the Latin American countries also differed with the level of the cultures encountered by the conquest. In Mexico and Upper Peru colonization entailed fusion with highly developed civilizations. In Argentina, Chile, Brazil, and the Caribbean, by contrast, the presence of less advanced cultures meant that more markedly Iberian societies evolved there. In Brazil and the Caribbean, the colonists later engaged in economic activities that required a large labour force, and slaves were imported from Africa, which introduced a third element into the pattern of cultural development.

At the time of independence, the administrative divisions of the colonial era were consolidated as national boundaries. The size and natural resources of these new nations were very disparate, and their topography varied from the high mountain ranges in the Andes to the deserts of northern Mexico and northern Chile, the vast savannahs of the Pampas in Argentina, and the equatorial rain forest of the Amazon basin. The natural barriers dividing Latin America obstructed intra-regional trade and the evolution of an integrated market. During the world economic boom that began in the mid-nineteenth century, each Latin American country established bilateral economic links with the then recently industrialized countries of the northern hemisphere.

The subsequent economic and social evolution of each country was greatly influenced by the size and composition of its trade with the industrialized countries. Pronounced contrasts emerged, for example, between countries that relied heavily on exports of minerals and those that specialized in exporting agricultural products. Nonetheless, the Latin American countries are no more diverse than those of Europe. For example, Sweden's level of development differs from that of Greece as much as Argentina's differs from that of Guatemala; Italy and Norway are divided by an economic, social, and cultural gap as wide as that separating Chile from Venezuela; even within the EEC, Luxembourg's economic potential compares as unfavourably with Germany's as does that of Honduras with that of Brazil. Moreover, Latin Americans think of and treat the region as having geographical and social unity.

Even so, though various economists and political groups have long propounded the necessity of union if the continent is to attain greater world standing, Latin America has made slow progress towards economic integration. In 1967, the Heads of American States resolved to 'create progressively, beginning in 1970, the Latin American Common Market, which shall be substantially in operation in a period of no more than fifteen years'. Almost 20 years had passed since the ECLA had launched the idea of a Latin American common market that would promote specialization in industrial production within the framework of an enlarged and protected regional market. However, despite advances in integration, intra-regional imports today amount to just over 14 per cent of total Latin American imports compared with the 11 per cent they represented in 1948.

Latin America and the European Economic Community:
Intra-Regional Imports as a Percentage of Total Imports

Year	Latin America (a)	EEC
1938	8	—
1948	11	—
1960	10	34
1964	13	40
1968	14	46
1970	13	48

(a) Excluding Cuba.
Source: IMF, *Direction of Trade*, and estimates for 1938 and 1948.

Long before integration was agreed on as a desirable scheme by Latin American governments, different types of trade and payments arrangements had been drawn up between Latin American countries. Barter deals were concluded during the war and early post-war years, such as those between Cuba and Ecuador in 1946 exchanging sugar for rice. Argentina, for example, maintained a policy, fostered since Spanish colonial times, of favouring trade with her neighbours by means of a preference scheme exempting these countries from the exchange controls that she imposed from the 1930s onwards. This was the case with imports from Paraguay, Bolivia, and Chile. With Brazil, there were, and still are, agreements mainly on trade in primary products, such as wheat, coffee, and fruit.

The foreign exchange reserves accumulated by Latin America during the Second World War, and the good prices for primary products that prevailed throughout the Korean War, obscured the need to integrate the economies of the region in order to avoid external difficulties. Because of this, import substitution was pursued separately by each country, and it was not until the end of the 1950s, when foreign exchange crises began to occur and short-term indebtedness began to grow, that integration was seriously seen as a necessity.

It became widely accepted in Latin America that productive possibilities were better suited to commercial competition within the region than to international trade; the countries of the region then agreed upon an integration process to overcome some of the deficiencies in the external sector by applying import substitution in a regional rather than a national context. Four distinct groupings now exist in the region. Their principal objectives are to establish a common market (Central American Common Market), two free trade areas (Latin American Free Trade Association, and Caribbean Free Trade Association), and an economic community (the Andean Group).

In the Central American Common Market (CACM), reciprocal trade had been largely liberalized before the war between El Salvador and Honduras in 1969 brought about an interruption of the process of integration; intra-Central American exports amounted to over 23 per cent of the total exports of the five countries. Moreover, not only had there been a great increase in the value of trade, but more than two-thirds of it had been in manufactures or semi-manufactures. This helped to rationalize the industrial structure, within the limitations of a regional market smaller than the individual markets of Colombia, Chile, or Peru, who are themselves trying to integrate to overcome the small size of their markets.

The objective of the countries that signed the Treaty of Montevideo in 1960, and of those that adhered to it later, was to establish a free trade area. The basic instrument for trade liberalization in the Latin American Free Trade Association (LAFTA) is annual negotiation among the member countries on tariff reductions for

Economic Indicators of Various Latin American Regional Groups in 1970

	Est. Population millions	Est. GDP ($ million)	Total Exports ($ million)	Exports to Countries within Group ($ million)	Exports within Group as % of Total Exports
CARIFTA	3.86	2,570	988	69	7
Barbados	0.24	140	46	8	17
Guyana	0.72	270	340	14	4
Jamaica	1.87	1,350	120	14	12
Trinidad and Tobago	1.03	810	482	33	7
CACM	15.06	6,900	1,113	258	23
El Salvador	3.44	1,500	223	68	31
Guatemala	5.28	2,400	295	95	32
Honduras	2.58	800	197	15	7
Nicaragua	2.02	900	171	34	20
Costa Rica	1.74	1,300	227	46	20
LAFTA	240.61	162,900	12,818	1,214	10
Argentina	24.35	29,500	1,773	366	21
Brazil	93.25	45,000	2,807	264	9
Bolivia	4.66	1,200	165	14	8
Chile	9.78	8,400	1,163	116	10
Colombia	22.16	10,300	777	77	10
Ecuador	6.03	2,500	303	30	10
Mexico	50.72	43,300	1,399	93	7
Peru	13.59	7,800	1,048	64	6
Paraguay	2.42	800	64	20	32
Uruguay	2.89	2,600	233	29	13
Venezuela	10.76	11,500	3,086	141	5
ANDEAN GROUP	56.22	30,200	3,456	119	4
Bolivia	4.66	1,200	165	2	1
Chile	9.78	8,400	1,163	17	1
Colombia	22.16	10,300	777	56	7
Ecuador	6.03	2,500	303	25	8
Peru	13.59	7,800	1,048	21	2

Sources: Based on material from LADC, ECLA, IMF, and UN.

specific products. Despite the limitations of such complex negotiation procedures, exports of LAFTA countries within the area have grown at a higher rate than those to the rest of the world. Though intra-regional trade started from a very low base, this pattern seems to indicate that it is easier to expand this type of trade than external trade.

Negotiations in LAFTA have reached a state of near stagnation, and some pessimists interpret the creation of the Andean Group in 1969 as an acknowledgement by the signatory countries of the Cartagena Agreement (Bolivia, Colombia, Chile, Ecuador, and Peru, joined in 1973 by Venezuela) of the failure of LAFTA.

The Cartagena Agreement sets a course of planned integration. The programme identifies various groups of products for each of which there are specific rules regarding the reduction and elimination of customs duties, and the gradual establishment of a common external tariff. The group that is perhaps most vital to the Agreement's objective of planned integration is that comprising products that will be involved in regional development plans for specific sectors of industry.

In 1968, the agreement setting up the Caribbean Free Trade Association (CARIFTA) was signed by four countries (Barbados, Guyana, Jamaica, and Trinidad and Tobago) and seven associated states (which together form the East Caribbean Common Market). The liberalization programme provides for the elimination by 1973 of all customs duties applicable to imports from the members of the zone, except for a limited number of products that are subject to progressive reduction. Furthermore, the treaty provides for a broad suppression of non-tariff barriers and in particular quantitative restrictions. Here, as in most aspects of the programme, the less developed territories have special advantages.

If these groups fulfil the commitments they have undertaken, within the periods laid down in their respective instruments, their various objectives will be reached between 1978 and 1985. However, the possibility of the four movements managing to unite to give integration a regional scope seems unlikely to materialize in the way envisaged by the Heads of State in 1967, unless further measures are taken at the political level.

The obstacles to integration have in fact multiplied. The inward-looking development policies of the Latin American countries have entailed heavy protection of national markets. Strong interests have ensconced themselves around industry that is often inefficient, and have baulked attempts to reduce protective barriers so as to increase regional trade. The region's failure to achieve greater economic integration in the past two decades is a direct result of the way in which the problems of semi-development have been tackled, and the priorities of development strategy selected.[6]

NOTES

[1] The long-term growth tendency of France's national product between 1830 and 1954 was one per cent; for Italy between 1860 and 1900 it was 1.7 per cent; and for the U.S.A. between 1869/78 and 1953, 1.8 per cent. See International Bank for Reconstruction and Development, Technical Secretariat, Statistics on Economic Development (Washington, D.C., 8 March 1956).

[2] In non-socialist Europe in 1960 the employment status of the total labour force was as follows: 75.3 per cent paid employees; 16.4 per cent employers and self-employed; and 8.3 per cent unpaid family workers. E. J. Hobsbawm, Industry and Empire (Harmondsworth: Penguin, 1969), p. 317.

[3] It is possible that the low population density of Latin America has been an important factor in the avoidance of armed hostility among its countries. In 1970 there were 14 people for every square kilometre, compared with 94 in Europe and 64 in South-East Asia.

[4] The major exception was the boundary between the United States and Mexico, which was fixed as a result of the annexation of Texas by the U.S.A. in 1845, the cession of New Mexico and Upper California in 1848 after the Mexican-American War, and the sale, under duress, in 1859 of La Mesilla, which later came to form part of Arizona.

[5] David Wood, Conflict in the Twentieth Century (London: Institute for Strategic Studies, Adelphi Paper No. 48, June 1968), pp. 24–6.

[6] For further discussion of the problems and prospects of regional integration, see Chapters 6 and 12.

Priorities of Development

Chapter 4

Problems of Growth and Development

Latin America is confronted by many difficult development problems; they are mainly economic, but also have intricate social and political implications. A high rate of population growth continues most persistently among the groups that are least equipped to cope with it and most afflicted by its consequences; the large migration of people from the countryside to the cities begets a combination of economic hardship, social despondency, and political volatility, each making it harder to tackle the others; unequal income distribution is maintained by entrenched political and social modes and inefficient social organization; unemployment and under-employment are generally high and need to be reduced not merely to relieve social distress, but also to make better use of productive capacity.

These problems have assumed serious proportions because growth has not proceeded fast enough in the post-war period, and because many of the measures to promote development have been misguided. Many economic policies pursued in Latin America have paid too little attention to, and at times have even obstructed, the modernization of agriculture and traditional industries. This has slowed down increases in the production of basic items of consumption, the supply of which has been inadequate for expanding populations. Furthermore, price distortions have occasioned rural depression and excessive urban concentration; an inordinate protection of industry has, directly or indirectly, raised the price of basic items of consumption and hampered the growth of exports; the slow growth of exports has in turn created import shortages, pushed up prices still further, and impeded overall growth; insufficient growth has led to increased unemployment and under-employment; regressive taxation and the high price of everyday necessities have reinforced inequitable income distribution.

Though Latin America's development problems are the effect, and the mismanagement of economic policies the cause, more consideration is often given to the problems than to the policies. This

49

has had two harmful consequences : in the first place, the problems have come to appear more intractable than they really are, and there has emerged a myth that development cannot proceed until such obstacles have been removed; second, preoccupation with the problems has diverted energy from the fundamental task facing Latin America, which is to revise its economic strategy so as to speed up growth. The problems are serious but not hopeless, and would be obviated if growth were rapid. This is true even for the apparently least soluble of them, such as population increases and income distribution.

I. POPULATION

The population problem in Latin America typifies the quandary in which semi-development places the region. Improved standards of hygiene and extensive public health measures have brought about an impressive drop in the death rate during the past 25 years. The birth rate, however, has remained more or less constant at a high figure, largely because the levels of education and the social attitudes that induce lower birth rates are not yet general in Latin America. As a result, there has been a rapid rise in the

Latin America: Birth and Death Rates per 1,000 inhabitants, 1900–1965

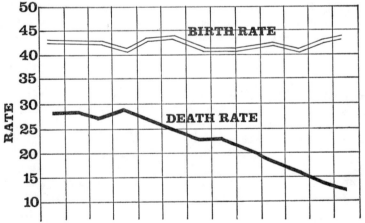

Source: ECLA, División de Asuntos Sociales, *La Situación Demográfica en América Latina,* July 1968 (unpublished).

region's population, and economic expansion has been inadequate to satisfy the inhabitants' growing needs.

At the beginning of the 1970s, Latin America, together with the few remaining dependencies of the United States and Europe, contains a population approaching 300 million, which is little more than 15 per cent higher than that of the enlarged European Economic Community. Its total area, somewhat greater than 20 million square kilometres, is about 11 times that of the enlarged European Community.

The population of Latin America is growing, however, at an overall rate of about 2.9 per cent a year, which is one of the highest in the world. The birth rate is significantly higher than that of Europe in the last century, and in many parts of the region is equivalent to that of some African and Asian countries. This high rate helps to accentuate inequalities in the distribution of income, because the increase is faster in the poorest regions and among the poorest groups in the Latin American countries. It also makes for a high proportion of dependent population, and so imposes an ever-increasing burden on social investment.

This burden is all the greater because the urban population is rising much faster than the rural population. In 1950, only 25 per cent of the total population inhabited cities, but by 1970 this proportion had risen above 40 per cent, and there were 220 cities of more than 100,000 inhabitants, of which 35 had a population exceeding 500,000. The process of migration from the country-side to urban centres, brought about by the relative advantages offered by cities in a situation of semi-development, is of a highly cumulative nature, and has caused social adjustment traumas resembling those experienced in Europe in the nineteenth century, and in the United States early in the twentieth. Accelerated urban agglomeration has resulted in slums appearing in and around all the big cities of the region. It is much more costly to improve the precarious living conditions of these communities than to provide for rural populations. Moreover, the level of social services expected in the Latin American countries has been set by the industrialized countries, which were themselves under no such constraint when they were passing through a period of fast population growth in the last century.[2]

The situation varies greatly from one country or region to another. In Haiti, Barbados, El Salvador, the central plateau of Mexico, and north-east Brazil, the rate of increase of population has already created intense pressure on resources that are still quite inadequate. In Venezuela and south-east Brazil, population pressure is still far from constituting an important obstacle to the development effort. In Argentina, where resources are abundant and relatively well developed, and the birth rate is low, there is no population problem.

The rapid post-war expansion of the population became a major concern in the early 1960s. It was pointed out that the rate of population growth was unprecedented in history, and that, though the space and natural resources of the region were ample, the capacity of the Latin American countries to utilize these assets was not equal to the needs of their inhabitants. Unfortunately, from this premise it has been falsely inferred that the Latin American countries are incapable of achieving economic development adequate to support and employ their expanding populations.

Were this pessimistic view valid, the outlook would indeed be gloomy. In the absence of satisfactory economic growth, the Latin American countries will remain for some decades, and perhaps indefinitely, unable to make adequate provision for their inhabitants, however effective may be government measures to bring about a voluntary reduction in fertility. No matter how widespread the introduction of family planning services, the results cannot be felt for some time. Both the slowing-down of the rate of increase and the change in the age composition of the population (to include a smaller proportion of young dependants) take effect only gradually. Even in Cuba, where the government has conducted a large-scale and very successful birth control policy in recent years, the economy is still overloaded by the size and structure of the population, and unless more rapid economic growth is achieved, this situation will continue until almost the end of the century.

The dismal prognoses of the 1960s should be weighed against the enormous unexploited areas and prodigious natural resources of the continent. The average net density of population is very low, in relation to both total area and potential agricultural land. This is particularly significant in view of the immense possibilities of increasing productivity afforded by the 'Green Revolution', and the advances in technology that make it practicable to open up deserts and jungles to economic exploitation. There is no doubt that, properly developed, the region's resources are more than sufficient to satisfy the needs of its population.[3] Even at the present rates of population growth, by the end of the century Latin America will have reached a population density only one-third that of Europe today.

By concentrating its efforts on development, Latin America cannot only make available enough of its resources to support its inhabitants, but can also provide a strong incentive to lowering the birth rate. Experience indicates that rapid development brings with it economic and social changes that induce parents to want fewer children.[4] It will be necessary for governments to respond to this tendency by ensuring that the bulk of the population has access to those birth control techniques already used by the middle and upper classes in Latin America, and to others that may be developed in the future.

That the population problem can best be solved by vigorous development was pointed out by the President of Mexico, Luis Echeverría, in a speech made in April 1972 at the UNCTAD III conference in Santiago :

> The rate of population increase will have to be reduced because it is in the interest of our peoples that it should be; but the primordial task ahead of us is to push vigorously and wholeheartedly towards development.

Population is a problem that requires action and not words. In the interests of national welfare, Latin American governments should take practical steps to help slow down the rate of population growth. Latin Americans should not accept the type of argument that confuses the present state of development with the region's potential capacity to maintain a larger population.

II. INCOME DISTRIBUTION

The feudal type of land tenure introduced with the conquest met with mounting opposition both from the Church, which was concerned for the well-being of the Indians, and from the Spanish and Portuguese crowns, which were anxious to maintain control over the territories of the New World. Despite this, the evolution of a colonial socio-economic organization, based largely on the exploitation of cheap manpower, resulted in a land tenure structure that retained some feudal characteristics, including a regressive distribution of income. Even after independence, large areas of land continued to be concentrated in a few hands. This pattern gave rise to social problems of major importance in the development of countries such as Peru, Chile, Colombia, and those of Central America; it was disrupted by revolutions in Mexico, Bolivia, and Cuba, and is being changed in differing degrees through agrarian reforms in many other Latin American countries.

The structure of land tenure has been modified also by the development process, which has brought about large-scale migration from the countryside to the towns, the transfer of rural estates to modern urban entrepreneurs who have developed capitalist agriculture, and rapid industrialization which has generated new middle groups.[5] Now that only 20 per cent of income is generated by the agricultural sector, even big landowners no longer receive an inordinate proportion of the national wealth. Nonetheless, the partly feudal system that existed up to the beginning of this century is still being used as a basis for discussing the distribution of income in Latin America, though the situation ought to be analysed from another viewpoint.

Comparisons of the distribution of money income before taxes among three income groups (the upper 5 per cent, the middle 45 per cent, and the lower 50 per cent) do not reveal significant differences between Latin America and the industrialized countries. It is unwise to infer too much from data of this sort, which are defective both for developed countries and for Latin America; they suggest, however, that the proportion of total personal income received by the poorest 50 per cent of the population in France, for example, is no greater than that received by the same group in Chile or Mexico, and substantially less than in Argentina; the higher overall level of incomes in France, however, enables the lowest income group to enjoy a higher standard of living than its equivalent in Chile and Mexico, and perhaps even in Argentina.[6]

In countries such as Britain, West Germany, or Sweden a much higher proportion of personal income passes to the poorest 50 per cent than is generally the case in Latin America. The share of personal income received by the next 45 per cent in Latin America throws into sharp relief the growth of the middle groups. For example, in Venezuela and in Chile the next 45 per cent receive about 60 per cent of all personal income. This is very simlar to the proportion in West Germany, though lower than in France or the United States, where undoubtedly the middle class is more firmly ensconced than it is in Latin America.

In Latin America as a whole, an excessive proportion of national income is received by the 5 per cent of the population in the highest income bracket, but it is worth noting that it is the same proportion (one-third) that the same group in the United States was receiving in the 1920s, when that country's economy was at a more advanced stage and its *per capita* g.n.p. was higher than that of Latin America today.[7]

More detailed statistics sometimes reveal extreme contrasts between different parts of a single country. In Brazil, for instance, average income in the south is more than twice as high as in the north, a situation comparable to that of Italy, where average income in the south is barely half that in Lombardy. There are also wide disparities between the real incomes of rural and urban areas, partly because prices of manufactured goods have risen faster than agricultural prices. Emigration to the cities tends to ease the problem in, for example, Mexico and Upper Peru.

The most far-reaching trend in income distribution in Latin America is the shift of income from the highest income bracket towards the middle groups. Material progress has brought with it growing social mobility. Significant middle groups have emerged, comprising organized labour, the professions, and independent entrepreneurs. Unlike the middle classes that were formed in Europe in the sixteenth and seventeenth centuries and in North America in the eighteenth and early nineteenth centuries, by developing trade and industry in the burgeoning towns, the middle groups in Latin America have to some extent been the product rather than the progenitors of development. Political parties today, whether of the Left or of the Right, cater largely for the aspirations of these middle groups, though they broaden their platforms to attract the urban and rural masses, mainly to gain votes and numerical strength. This political process has gone so far that it has even permeated traditionalist institutions like the Church and the armed forces.

The strength of the middle groups has increased as a consequence of educational opportunities and the process of urban-industrial development. Their advancement has been reinforced by their close association with the growth of comprehensive government bureaucracies which have promoted fiscal policies that serve, primarily, the short-term interests of the middle groups, and place them in a more favourable position than their counterparts in most developed countries. Not only do the middle groups in Latin America gain more than the poorer groups from government transfers in the form of social security plans, housing, education, and so forth, but a disproportionate load of taxation is saddled on the poorer groups by tax systems that still rely excessively on indirect taxation.[8] The table below illustrates the situation in Colom-

Tax Incidence by Income Group in Colombia

Income Groups (*1000 pesos p.a.*)	Direct Taxes	Indirect Taxes	All Taxes
	PERCENTAGES OF INCOME		
0–3	1.47	11.18	12.8
6–10	3.98	8.96	14.0
40–80	7.79	7.84	16.4
200 plus	11.29	5.54	16.8
TOTAL	5.50	8.10	14.1

Source: Felix Paukert, 'Sécurité Sociale et Redistribution du Revenu; Etude Comparée' in *Revue Internationale du Travail*, XCVIII, 5 November 1968.

bia in 1968, where the proportion of government revenue derived from direct taxes was higher than in most Latin American countries. Even there, however, the incidence of indirect taxes on the poor was so high that they bore a tax burden almost equal to that imposed on the richer groups.

The state of semi-development affords the middle groups advantages that enable them to increase their share of the national income, which they generally do to the detriment of public and private savings and of the advancement of the poorest sectors. Latin American governments have taken steps to improve income distribution, with positive effects in some cases. In Uruguay, for example, income distribution is better than in some European countries, as a result of the massive social legislation enacted since the 1920s. In Venezuela the distribution of personal income, calculated on the basis of national income, is probably better than in other developing countries because the state plays an important role in distributing income through taxes levied on export proceeds received by foreign petroleum companies.

There is, however, a limit to what social and fiscal measures can achieve if a country's development effort falls short; the serious economic and political difficulties that Uruguay is now experiencing are a cogent demonstration of this. While semi-development lasts, income distribution will continue to militate against the poor. Because of low agricultural productivity and poor marketing, the 40 per cent of Latin America's labour force engaged in rural activities are poorly rewarded and, because of inefficient industrialization, the urban poor can find work, if at all, only in personal services and badly paid occupations generally. The same structural defects of agriculture and industry result in excessively high prices for food products and basic industrial items of consumption, on which poor families must spend most of their income. Semi-development not only restricts the income and raises the expenditure of poor people, but also often leads to conditions of inflation and unemployment that further worsen their situation.

Until a modern and efficient system of production is set up, imbalances in the distribution of real income are likely to remain. Policies aimed at redistributing income can have little effect if there is not enough production to distribute. Only more rapid growth can, at the same time, generate more and higher paid employment, provide cheaper and better quality food products and consumer goods, and ensure a greater degree of economic stability.

The semi-development achieved by the Latin American countries provides them with the basis for rapid further development during the coming decades. Hitherto the economic successes achieved and the social changes experienced have often been overshadowed by the social conflicts engendered by the development process. A vicious circle has been created in which social tensions and their political manifestations have made it increasingly hard to devise economic policies that would enable the Latin American countries to embark upon a self-sustaining development process.

If the countries of the region are not to vegetate in a mediocre fashion, they must adopt strategies to distinguish problems that are symptomatic of the state of semi-development from the fundamental problem of constructing an efficient production system to enable the region to progress beyond that state. As long as Latin America remains semi-developed, problems such as rapid population growth, overcrowding in cities, unfair income distribution, and unemployment will remain endemic, and solutions will be merely partial or short-lived. Latin America cannot safely neglect any of these problems, but it will solve them only by striving to end the state of semi-development. This it can do only by giving priority, within an overall development strategy, to an adequate expansion of production.[9] If Latin America does not place its problems in their proper perspective, it runs the risk of failing to solve any of them.

There could arise the paradox of the region indulging in frantic political activity, only to be left at the end of the century with a modest *per capita* income. Those who would suffer most from such a turn of events would be the poor, who, though less prone than other Latin Americans to philosophize about development, are those who are most genuinely concerned that it should come about, and should result not in a society of this or that type, but in their having greater access to more and better goods and services.

NOTES

[1] *United Nations Demographic Yearbook 1970* (New York, 1971).

[2] The industrialized countries of Europe also benefited from the safety valve of emigration. Between 1840 and 1940 more than 60 million Europeans emigrated, almost a quarter of them to Latin America.

[3] 'There is no technical reason why agricultural output cannot be raised from the current rate of increase of 2–3 per cent to 4 or even 5 per cent a year... However, technology will have to change with more emphasis on increasing output per unit of input rather than on increasing traditional inputs without raising the productivity of those inputs'. Montague Yudelman, with Frederic Howard, *Agricultural Development and Economic Integration in Latin America* (London: Allen & Unwin, 1970), p. 36.

[4] See T. Paul Schultz, 'An Economic Perspective on Population Growth' in National Academy of Sciences, *Rapid Population Growth. Consequences and Policy Implications* (Baltimore, Md.: Johns Hopkins, 1971), also published as RAND Paper P–4607 (Santa Monica, Calif.: RAND Corporation, July 1971).

[5] The capitalist nature of Latin American agriculture is recognized by Marxist economists such as André Gunder Frank: 'The Brazilian economy, including its agriculture, is part of a capitalist system. It is the development and functioning of this system which produce both development and under-development and which account for the terrible reality of agriculture in Brazil – and elsewhere'. André Gunder Frank, *Capitalism and Underdevelopment in Latin America: Historical Studies of Chile and Brazil* (Harmondsworth: Penguin, 1971), p. 240.

[6] The figures given in this and the following paragraph are taken from 'Incomes in Post-War Europe: a Study of Policies, Growth and Distribution' in *Economic Survey of Europe in 1965: Part II* (Geneva: United Nations, 1967); *The Economic Development of Latin America in the Post-War Period* (New York: United Nations, 1964).

[7] See Colin Bradford Jr, *Forces for Change in Latin America: US Policy Implications* (Washington D.C.: Overseas Development Council, 1971), and John Kenneth Galbraith, *The Great Crash 1929* (Harmondsworth: Penguin, 1969), pp. 194–5.

[8] According to ECLA, in 1966, indirect taxes represented 49 per cent of all taxes in Argentina, 62 per cent in Brazil, 40 per cent in Chile, 54 per cent in Guatemala, and 37 per cent in Mexico.

[9] Experience convinced the Soviet Union, after the first few years of the New Economic Policy, that the expansion of production was the principal problem to be resolved. Consequently, the question was handled pragmatically by Stalin, on the basis of Trotsky's and Preobrazhensky's economic theses.

Chapter 5

Industrialization and Production

ⅠAᴛ ᴛʜᴇ ʀᴏᴏᴛ ᴏғ Latin America's deficient economic performance in the post-war period has been a development strategy that has failed to emphasize efficient production. No long-range industrial policy was formulated to ensure reasonable and stable conditions that would encourage conscientious entrepreneurs and facilitate the development of efficient industry. Instead, domestic production was excessively protected by various means (exchange controls, quantitative restrictions, tariffs, and so forth); this was an easy way to encourage local production of goods that had formerly been imported, and it enabled the Latin American countries to attain apparently satisfactory growth rates of their g.d.p. and to increase the proportion of industrial production in their g.d.p. from about 19 per cent in 1950 to slightly over 25 per cent in 1970.

Share of the Industrial Product in the Total Gross Domestic Product

(percentages)

	1950	*1960*	*1970*
Argentina	29.4	32.2	35.3
Brazil	15.1	21.4	24.7
Chile	21.2	23.7	n. a.
Mexico	19.9	23.3	27.0
Latin America	18.7	21.7	25.2

Source: ECLA, *Industrial Development in Latin America* E/CN/12/830 (Santiago, 13 March 1969), p. 5, Table 1, and private National Statistics.

However, the level of industrialization and its impact on the economy appear more modest when industrial production is valued at international rather than at the high internal prices. Two examples, among many that could be cited, illustrate this point. It has been calculated that the cost incurred by Chile through the misdirected allocation of resources, resulting from the policy of industrial protection, is equivalent to 10 per cent of the national income.[1] Similarly, the value of industrial production in Mexico in

1967 would be about 25 per cent less, which would noticeably reduce its proportion to the total product.[2]

It has been said of the industrial structure of the socialist countries of eastern Europe that it is 'prematurely old'.[3] This phrase refers to the fact that, even when this structure resembles that of the other industrialized countries, industrial specialization is inadequate, production is on too small a scale, and the machinery is antiquated. A similar description could apply to many sectors of Latin American industry, even though, in some cases, the machinery may be more modern than that of the socialist countries.

In the market economies of Latin America this state of affairs is usually reflected in the fact that industrial prices are substantially higher than those prevailing in world markets. High costs have hampered exports of manufactures and have imposed on the Latin American economies a permanent 'external gap'. From the internal point of view, the three most serious consequences of this type of industrialization – based on import substitution without considera-tion of the economic cost[4] – have been a sluggish development of agriculture, the consolidation and perpetuation of an inadequate distribution of income, and the neglect of technology.

I. AGRICULTURE

Industrialization policies have in effect been forcing agriculture partly to subsidize the development process.[5] For this reason, the agricultural potential of Latin America is still far from being ful-filled. Twenty-five per cent of the surface area is used for pasture, but only 6 per cent is land under cultivation. This could be greatly expanded, especially in view of recent technological advances, in-cluding new techniques in tropical agriculture. Yields are generally very low by comparison with those of the industrialized countries, and they could be much improved by increasing irrigation and the use of fertilizers, and particularly by extensively adopting the new strains that have been developed in the 'Green Revolution' in Mexico.

Whereas the real contribution of industry to g.d.p. is often over-stated, that of agriculture is probably underestimated because agricultural prices are relatively lower than industrial prices, and because the production not marketed by farmers is not always re-corded in national account statistics. The following table is, never-theless, illustrative of some of the varied problems confronting agriculture in different countries of the region.

A reduction in the proportion of the work force engaged in

Agriculture: Work Force Employed and GDP Generated 1968
(percentages)

	Work Force	GDP
Guatemala	64	27
Brazil	46	19
Mexico	46	12
Colombia	45	32
Chile	26	9
Venezuela	25	7
Latin America	43	17

Source: IDB Statistical Section. Reproduced in Inter-American Development Bank, *Socio-Economic Progress in Latin America. Social Progress Trust Fund Tenth Annual Report 1970* (Washington, D.C., 1971), pp. 6-7.

agriculture does not necessarily lead to increased general productivity within the sector if agriculture has been stagnant, as in Chile, or growing inadequately, as in Venezuela. In Colombia and Guatemala general productivity is not so low because of the importance of the agricultural export sector.

The productivity of the agrarian sector, compared with the rest of the economy, is very low in both Brazil and Mexico, though for different reasons. In Brazil, it is another instance of regional disparities; the agricultural situation in São Paulo and Rio Grande do Sul is quite satisfactory, but rural unemployment and underemployment in the north-east result in very low productivity for the country as a whole.

In Mexico, the low productivity is due to the large number of landless agricultural workers, who represented over 50 per cent of the active agricultural population at the beginning of the 1960s.[6] Their plight has arisen to a large extent because of the lack of good agricultural land, and the heavy investments needed for irrigation schemes to make more land cultivable.

Argentina maintains relatively high agricultural productivity, because a large part of agricultural production (both livestock and crops) is geared to exports. Throughout Latin America there is a marked contrast between the often efficient and modern production of plantation agricultural commodities for export, such as cotton in Nicaragua and Mexico, and the undercapitalized and inefficient nature of much of the agricultural production for internal consumption, which is apparent in the still inadequate irrigation facilities and the insignificant use of fertilizers in comparison with the developed regions.

Apart from production for export, agriculture has developed most satisfactorily in the medium-sized private farms supplying

Use of Commercial Fertilizer per Hectare, kilogrammes

Japan	410
Western Europe	162
North America	70
Latin America	21
Africa	3

Source: Food and Agriculture Organization, *The State of Food and Agriculture* (Rome, 1971), p. 31.

urban centres, though there have also been many examples of technically competent co-operative efforts in the *ejidos* (traditional communal farms) in Mexico, and in co-operative and state farms in Chile, Cuba, and more recently in Peru. In Latin America as a whole, however, the increase in agricultural production has only more or less kept pace with the growth in population. In the case of agriculture for internal consumption, this is because the sector has been undercapitalized during the post-war period, and has in many cases been subject to disincentive price controls.

The lack of vitality in the more modern sector of agriculture for export, on the other hand, is attributable as much to the state of international demand as to internal policy. In effect, the post-war patterns of international trade in foodstuffs have constituted a serious obstacle to an expansion of production in regions of Latin America which have an enormous agricultural potential. Unstable prices, restrictions and discrimination against imports, and the policy of self-sufficiency pursued by the advanced countries (for example, the EEC Common Agricultural Policy) are not conducive to the formulation of long-term policies by exporting countries.

As experience has demonstrated, especially in the past ten years, there are no simple policy solutions in agriculture; many of the economic factors that have resulted in a lower rate of growth of production than was to be expected are intertwined with social problems deriving from the structure of land tenure. Furthermore, failure to distinguish between investment directed to social purposes and that geared to the productive effort, which has often occurred in the past decade, has served only to confuse the agricultural situation in Latin American countries.

In many instances, land redistribution is economically necessary and socially indispensable, though it is not in itself always sufficient to increase production. Smallholdings, which concentrate a large number of landowners or tenants on a small proportion of the total agricultural land, and latifundia, which denote a small number of landowners owning a high proportion of the land, are still widespread phenomena. Because of intensive cultivation, yields per acre in smallholdings are generally higher than those prevailing in latifundia conditions. On the other hand, yields per worker are higher in the large estates, which implies that the techniques in use are adequate for extensive farming.

The redistribution of land to achieve a better land-to-worker relationship should, in some circumstances, produce positive results. First, by alleviating the pressure on land within the smallholding sector, it should help to reduce migration to the cities. Second, it would tend to raise the productivity of land by the sheer application of labour to it. However, as repeated agrarian experiments in Latin America have shown, a significant increase in production will come about only if redistribution of land is accompanied by credit facilities, extension services, and better marketing organizations.

In some cases, such as in Bolivia, Chile, and more recently Peru, land redistribution has been achieved effectively by agrarian reform providing for the expropriation of estates and direct assignment of land and water facilities to the peasants. Another method, perhaps not as appealing as land reform but just as effective, and certainly suited to conditions prevailing in many parts of Latin America, is land taxation designed to make it unprofitable to hold idle or unproductive estates.

One basic policy measure needed to procure a better rate of agricultural expansion is an improvement in the terms of trade between agricultural products and manufactures. There should be a bigger allocation of investment to agriculture, which could reduce social investment needs in the cities by slowing down the rate of urban immigration. Well-framed policies could also help to lower unemployment; it is comparatively easy to employ unskilled labour in productive agricultural tasks, provided that the cultivation methods used increase the productivity per acre without decreasing the manpower employed. Furthermore, there are plentiful possibilities of employment in other rural activities, such as road-making and own-home-building, which can also contribute to social welfare.

II. INDUSTRY

It is essential to expand agricultural production, but, as is shown by the experience of other countries with a large agricultural and mineral base, such as Australia and Canada, Latin America could not, and cannot, seriously contemplate economic development without industrialization.

To provide the employment and produce the manufactured goods that the population requires, Latin America needs light industry, intermediate industry, and heavy industry; the general industrial structure should be such that it helps to transfer the benefits of technological progress to the large masses of the population, and contributes to external financial independence through an increase in trade. In the post-war period the error lay not in the decision to accelerate industrialization, but in the way the issue was approached.

The pattern of international trade that evolved after the Second World War did not warrant the adoption of inward-looking development strategies to reproduce the conditions of 'enforced protection' that had prevailed during the Depression and the war. The region's earlier industrial achievements provide ample proof that Latin America could have taken advantage of the expansion of international trade in manufactures.

Industrialization in Latin America is not a post-war phenomenon. The region's export industries, such as sugar in both Brazil and Cuba, were among the first in the world to incorporate the technology of steam. In 1837, twelve years after the first steam railway opened in Britain, and seven years after the first in the United States, one was installed in Cuba, between Güines and Havana in an important sugar-producing district. By the turn of the century, the most advanced forms of production were to be found all over Latin America.

Mexico achieved industrial pre-eminence in Latin America during the first decade of this century. The Compañía Fundidora de Fierro y Acero de Monterrey began production of iron and steel in 1903 in what was the first major integrated iron and steel works in Latin America. At the same period, Mexico already had a textile industry of more than 20,000 looms with 700,000 spindles, employing more than 30,000 people, with equipment that in general matched the most advanced technology of the period.[7]

In Argentina and Brazil, the only other Latin American countries with a considerable economic potential, the industrial situation was no less promising. The iron and steel works of São Pao de Ipanema was one of the first in the American continent.[8] By 1920 the census recorded more than 13,000 industrial establishments in Brazil, the average establishment in São Paulo employing more than 20 people. The value of industrial production in São Paulo doubled in real terms between 1914 and 1920 and production per person employed increased at an annual rate of 4 per cent between 1920 and 1940.[9]

In Argentina, 'the average rate of growth in the manufacturing sector was greater in the period between the turn of the century and the Depression, than between then and the beginning of the 1960s'.[10] As early as 1895 the census recorded 22,204 manufacturing establishments, 2,348 steam engines, 31,700 industrial machines of other kinds, and about 150,000 people employed in the sector. In 1910 large industrial sectors already existed, among which was metallurgy. The industry was organized in large units; employing thousands of workers and using Siemens-Martin blast furnaces. About one-third of the country's internal requirements of farm machinery were being supplied by domestic industry, and railway equipment was being constructed in the country. Later, in about 1930, an oil refinery was installed that had been manufactured almost entirely within the country.

Industrialization was also taking place in the medium-sized countries of the region, such as Colombia and Peru, even if to a lesser extent. In Chile, for example, the rate of manufacturing expansion during the years 1914 to 1929 is calculated to have run at an annual cumulative rate of some 4.8 per cent.[11] Among the non-traditional industries then developing were ceramics and glassware, metallurgy and metal-transforming, and textiles, all of which were expanding at a rate of some 7 per cent annually.[12]

There is no lack of evidence to show that the degree and pace of industrial development in the years before the Depression of the 1930s were, by any standard, satisfactory. Immigration and a flourishing export sector probably provided great impetus to industrial development in the early part of the century; throughout the Latin American economies there was a surge of activity that created a sizeable demand for manufactures. This was increasingly satisfied by internal supply as the region largely followed the general tendency to establish light industries round the centres of consumption, which were already growing rapidly in the region.[13] Since there was little heavy industry, these light industries (basically foodstuffs, beverages, and textiles) together with the maintenance shops of transport and communications services, were the main source of the type of workshop activity and mechanical skills that had been the origin of intermediate and heavy industry in Britain during the industrial revolution, and were to be decisive in the development of the more basic industries that were set up in Brazil, Argentina, and Mexico after the Second World War.

Except for isolated cases, such as the deliberately protectionist measures favouring industry that were enacted in Chile from 1897,

C

no special steps were taken directly to encourage industry. There was a certain amount of indirect protection, which took several forms : the high cost of transporting manufactured goods made it generally cheaper to produce them locally than to import them; domestic industry was able to operate economically by establishing its production and marketing organization in the expanding urban centres; finally, tariffs imposed originally for purely fiscal purposes had the secondary effect of making imports more costly. Without these marginal advantages Latin American industry would have been much less able to face external competition during the period before the Depression. There are good grounds for the assertion of a Latin American economist that it

> would be erroneous to characterize the development process of all the Latin American countries in the period before the Depression by the absence of industrial growth. The common feature was not this. It was rather the non-existence of an industrialization policy.[14]

By the 1950s the growing complexity of production processes and technological advances, and the rising minimum scale of operations for economic production, meant that if the Latin American countries were to set up efficient industrial patterns, they would have to adopt comprehensive policies, comprising adequate levels of protection, regional integration, training, technological development, and, above all, the promotion of local entrepreneurs. In contrast with the ideal, each country has in fact resorted to excessive and inappropriate protection as a means of encouraging the installation within its borders of the full range of industries.

These policies have affected income distribution in Latin America; industries that produce on too small a scale to be economic have been able to pass on their high costs, and industries where the size of operations is unimportant have been able to reap high profits. Both high costs and high profits are felt by the consumer in the form of high prices.

Excess profits have to some extent become enforced savings to finance further industrialization. Easy profits have, however, allowed poor administrative standards to take root in firms in both the public and the private sectors, which have resulted in economic waste. Supposedly scarce capital resources have been squandered by using industrial plants far below their capacity.[15] This under-utilization of capacity has been accentuated in many instances by the recurrent crises arising from external weakness. Periods of expansion have led to inflation and excessive imports, and have been followed by policies of anti-inflationary restrictions and economic contraction. This has been the case of Argentina, where plant utilization has fluctuated around 75 per cent in the past 15 years, in comparison with 90 per cent in developed countries.

For industries such as foodstuffs, textiles, and footwear, over-protection has minimized the inducements to introduce plants specializing in particular goods and processes. These industries were classified as 'vegetative industries' by ECLA in its early studies during the 1950s, because in conditions of unchanging income distribution, the demand for their products grows slowly. This has meant that their access to industrial financing has been less than it might have been, and consequently their equipment is, for the most part, outdated or even obsolescent. This was, for example, the case of the textile industry in the middle of the last decade.

Textile Industry: Indicative Indices of the Level of Modernization of Machinery–newest equipment: 100

	COTTON Spinning Mills	WOOL Textile Mills
Argentina	49	34
Brazil	21	38
Colombia	91	73
Peru	31	25

Source: ECLA, *Process of Industrial Development*, p. 94.

This situation, with certain exceptions (such as in Colombia, where there has been a major renewal of the textile industry), has raised the general level of costs above those of a country such as the United States, even though wages tend to be lower in Latin America. Uncompetitive prices have hindered the export of these manufactures. Despite a recent increase in exports of manufactures from Brazil to the United States, Latin America still supplies only a very small proportion of the industrial goods imported into the United States, though in the manufacture of footwear, for example, a country such as Argentina has a much greater incipient advantage than the main suppliers, Italy, the South-East Asian countries, and more recently Spain.

Internally, neglect of the 'vegetative industries' has prolonged a state of maldistribution of real income that could have begun to improve with a reduction in prices and a wider availability of basic necessities, as happened earlier in the developed countries. Furthermore, domestically owned firms and local entrepreneurs, which from the beginning of the century bore the brunt of developing this sector of manufacturing, have been adversely affected, and placed at a disadvantage regarding foreign investment, by the absence of policies for fostering these industries.

From the point of view of income distribution, irrational protection and substitution policies in the so-called 'dynamic industries' have less serious consequences, because here high prices and poor quality, especially in durable consumer goods, are felt most by the middle groups whose emergence was promoted by the import substitution process itself, and who have in good measure benefited from its fruits. In other respects, the consequences are certainly more serious.

The available information suggests that the foreign ownership of industry increased not so much as a result of take-overs of existing firms as by the establishment of new plants in the substitutive branches of 'dynamic industry', and also in some cases by the precipitate way in which this substitution was brought about.[16] The need for technological skills in the development of 'dynamic industries' would probably in any case have entailed a large-scale foreign involvement, but had policies been more judicious and truly nationalist, they would have prompted broader participation by local investors and entrepreneurs in the development of these industries. Furthermore, carefully framed policies would have made it difficult for foreign companies to avoid making more than a minimal contribution to general economic welfare, as they have been able to do under irrational import substitution schemes.

A brief review of the situation in some of the 'dynamic industries' will serve to point out the ill-effects of rashly conceived policies. In the motor vehicle industry, production is normally economic only if a manufacturer is producing at least 250,000 units a year. With the exception of the Volkswagen plant in Brazil, which in 1971 produced over 300,000 units, and Fiat in Argentina, which has based its plans on the lines of a complex for motor vehicles, tractors, railway equipment, and diesel engines (but whose costs are still high), Latin America remains very far from this goal. In every country total motor vehicle production is below the minimum economic scale, yet it is distributed among many plants (10 in Argentina with a total production of less than 300,000 units, 7 in Mexico with about 200,000 units, and 13 in Peru with an output below 17,000 units), which assemble a disproportionate number of different models (120 in Venezuela). The industry can only be described as poorly planned.[17]

Annual production in the whole of Latin America exceeds a million units; the industry could be more efficiently organized if production were organized on a regional basis. And if Brazil,

Argentina, and Mexico became the Detroits of Latin America, they would certainly be able to make concessions to the Latin American Delawares which, for their part, could do very well.

A similar situation obtains in the basic and intermediate industrial sectors that supply the manufactured materials needed by the rest of industry. The chemical industry, of crucial importance in supplying material for manufactured goods, is among those industries that have been 'substituted' with the most fervour and the highest degree of protection in the post-war period. Over-protection has brought about a situation where the same process is duplicated in numerous plants whose average size is consistently lower than the minimum economic capacity that the technology of the industry now requires; for only a few products are there plants of an appropriate size in Latin America.

Chemical Industry: Annual Production Capacity for Selected Products
(thousands of tons)

Product	Latin America (existing plants)		Industrialized countries	
	Range of capacity	Average capacity (*1965/66*)	Economic capacity (*est.*)	Maximum capacity*
Sulphuric acid	5–100	40	100	700
Ammonia	8–132	50	200	450
Calcium carbide	4–36	23	50	300
Polyvinyl chloride	3–20	15	50	85
Polyethylene	10–30	20	20	200
Carbon black	7–33	18	15	80
Ethylene	8–54	26	150	450
Sodium carbonate	38–135	70	160	840
Methanol	12–16	13	60	190

* Order of magnitude, includes projects under way in 1968.
Source: ECLA, *Industrial Development in Latin America* E/CN/12/830 (Santiago, 13 March 1969), p. 28, Table 7.

The iron and steel industry, mainstay of the whole engineering industry, where the participation of private foreign investment has been much less and the direct responsibility of the Latin American governments much greater, also suffers from the consequences of small-scale production. The resulting high costs in basic industries are translated into greater inefficiency in other sectors of industry. It goes without saying that basic industries should be established in Latin America, but it is absurd to propose that they

be installed with total disregard for economic size and for investment and production costs. Latin America can develop competent
basic industries, and indeed it must do so, since they are the foundation on which to construct a modern and efficient productive
system.

To reach this goal, the Latin American countries will need to
change their industrial policies. They could learn much from study-
ing the experience of the smaller industrialized nations of Europe.
The European countries with a value of industrial production
similar to that of the largest Latin American countries have
achieved a higher degree of industrial efficiency through greater
specialization in production.

Value of Industrial Production in 1967* ($ million)

LATIN AMERICA	
Argentina	7,000
Brazil	6,800
Chile	1,600
Colombia	1,400
Mexico	6,900
EUROPE	
Austria	3,400
Belgium	5,400
Netherlands	6,500
Sweden	7,000

Source : ECLA, *La Política Industrial de América Latina*, E/CN/12/877.
United Nations, *Yearbook of National Account Statistics*, 1969 (New York, 1970) for
the European countries.

* If the value of industrial production of the Latin American countries
were calculated at international prices rather than at real internal cost, it
would be noticeably less.

More important still, because they specialize in comparatively
few products, these smaller countries manufacture in excess of
their internal consumption needs and rely in good measure on
exports to international markets. They are therefore selling largely
to a buyers' market which obliges them to produce cheaper and
better-quality goods, and to develop a high capacity for absorbing
and innovating technology. If the Latin American countries wish
to emulate this example, and to make better use of their resources,
they will also need to review the entire range of economic policies
and procedures that have grown up around the development
strategies of the post-war period.

NOTES

[1] Bela Balassa, 'Resource Allocation and Economic Integration in Latin America', paper given at Conference on 'The Next Decade of Latin American Development', Cornell University, April 1966, and published as 'Integración regional y asignación de recursos en América Latina', *Comercio Exterior* (September 1966).

[2] Nacional Financiera, *La Política Industrial en el Desarrollo Económico de México*, p. 38.

[3] Béla Kádár, *Gazdaságfejlesztés és nemzetközi munkamegosztas a fejlodo országokban* (Budapest, 1967), quoted in Bela Balassa, 'Growth Strategies in Semi-Industrial Countries', *Quarterly Journal of Economics*, LXXXIV, 1 (February 1970), p. 45.

[4] 'The criterion by which the choice was determined was based not on considerations of economic expediency but on immediate feasibility, whatever the cost of production'. Raúl Prebisch, *Towards a Dynamic Development Policy for Latin America* (New York: United Nations, 1964), p. 71.

[5] Bela Balassa, 'Regional Integration and Trade Liberalization in Latin America', in *Journal of Common Market Studies*, X, 1 (September 1971), p. 63.

[6] See *Censo Agrícolo Ganadero y Ejidal 1960*, Secretaría de Industria y Comercio.

[7] ECLA, *The Process of Industrial Development in Latin America*, E/CN.12/716/Rev. 1 (New York, 1966), p. 8.

[8] *La Economía Siderurgica de América Latina*. ECLA, LAISEP, IDB Joint Programme on the Integration of Industrial Development, Document EICN/12/727, February 1968.

[9] Warren Dean, *The Industrialization of Sao Paulo 1880–1945*, pp. 92 and 106.

[10] Andrés Bianchi, 'Notas sobre la teoría del desarrollo económico latinoamericano', Introduction to *América Latina: ensayos de interpretación económica* (Mexico: Siglo XXI), published separately as CIENES/5231 (150), 19 October 1967, p. 23.

[11] Oscar Muñoz, *Long-run Trends in the Manufacturing Industry in Chile since 1914* (University of Yale, unpublished doctoral thesis, 1969).

[12] Carlos Hurtado, *Concentración de población y desarrollo económico: el caso chileno* (Santiago: Instituto de Economía de la Universidad de Chile, Publicación No. 89, 1966), p. 92 and table 25.

[13] 'In Argentina, even before the First World War, more than half the population was classified as urban . . . By 1920, there were at least six towns in Brazil whose population amounted to more than 100,000 persons . . . In 1930, one third of the population of Mexico was living in urban centres, among which the Federal District alone had an urban population of over one million. The population of Buenos Aires already numbered more than one and a half million in 1914; by 1920, that of Rio de Janeiro exceeded one million, while Sao Paulo and Santiago, Chile, each had more than 500,000 inhabitants'. ECLA, *Process of Industrial Development*, p. 6.

[14] Andrés Bianchi, 'Notes sobre la teoría del desarrollo económico latinoamericano', p. 34.

[15] In order to avoid this kind of secondary consequence, a more direct form of channelling savings is preferable. In Mexico the Nacional Financiera has, to a good measure, come to be used for this purpose.

[16] A good example of the policy of substitution at all costs was provided by the Argentinian 'developmentists' who in 1958 approved the installation of 21 car factories.

[17] See Jack Baranson, *Automotive Industries in Developing Countries*. World Bank Staff Occasional Papers No. 8 (Washington, D.C.: IBRD, distributed by Johns Hopkins Press, 1969), p. 31.

Chapter 6

The Effective Use of Resources

THE LATIN AMERICAN countries urgently need to frame development strategies that stress efficiency of production, so that they may grow faster, export more, and further the process of regional integration. The inward-looking development strategies of the post-war period have impeded the execution of economic policy while making additional demands on it. The deficiencies of the productive system have progressively distorted the market machinery, and have thus made it increasingly necessary to manage the economies through administrative decisions. The same deficiencies, by preventing exports from growing faster, by allowing industrial goods to be overpriced, and by holding back the expansion of food production, have imposed fresh burdens on economic policy in the form of inflation, a heavy external debt, unemployment, and other obstacles. Because of the encumbrances placed on economic policy, the capital that has accrued from the process of semi-development, and the improvement in the ability of the work force, have not yielded the returns that were to be expected.

I. INVESTMENT AND HUMAN RESOURCES

In general, the Latin American countries can mobilize the physical resources and generate the savings necessary to achieve much higher rates of growth than those reached in the past decade. By the end of the 1960s investment represented about 20 per cent of the Latin American domestic product, a higher proportion than that prevailing in other developing regions, with the exception of southern Europe. Furthermore, Latin American countries were financing this investment with internal savings to a larger extent than the other developing regions.

The high proportion of investment to g.d.p., which is almost as large as in the industrialized countries, is rather deceptive. It is overestimated because of price distortions, in particular those that

72

Gross Investment and Savings as a Percentage of
Gross Domestic Product – Average for 1966–68

Region	Investment	Savings	Savings to Investment Ratio
Latin America	19.3	17.6	91
Argentina	18.9	19.7	104
Brazil	20.0	19.0	95
Colombia	19.0	15.9	84
Mexico	21.7	19.0	87
Africa	16.1	14.2	88
South Asia	15.3	12.4	81
Southern Europe	23.5	20.4	87
Industrialized countries	21.6	22.2	103

Source: Inter-American Development Bank, *Socio-Economic Progress in Latin America. Social Progress Trust Fund Tenth Annual Report 1970*, p. 45.

stem from the high prices of certain machinery and materials produced internally, and the costs caused by delays in completion of indispensable infrastructure and by inefficient public services.

Besides being overestimated, investment has not always been allocated by either the public or the private sector in such a way as to maximize growth, benefit the lower income groups, or reduce external financial dependence. For one thing, there has generally been an exaggerated allocation of investment to housing, especially for the upper and middle income groups. For another, because of pressures arising from urban immigration, investments in infrastructure have been concentrated too much in urban public works, which, unlike projects such as the construction of rural roads or the installation of dams for irrigation and hydroelectric plants, contribute only marginally to increasing production.

Investment in Latin America is both lower in real value than the figures suggest and less productive than better allocation would have allowed. Other factors, such as the demand of select groups of trade unions for disproportionately high wages, and the frequent subsidizing of capital through over-valued exchange rates, low interest rates, the waiving of duty on imports of machinery, and tax exemptions, tend to make industries over-capitalized and to make the import content of the investment unnecessarily large.

Were it not for these shortcomings the present rate of investment could be combined with greater use of the manpower available to increase g.d.p. at a faster pace. Bad allocation of investment has seriously limited its yield, and kept human resources unemployed when they could have been working productively.

Unless a larger part of this investment is steered towards production for export, it is useless to try to achieve an increase in investment, because directly or indirectly it adds to the demand for
imports. When the lack of external resources restricts the amount
that a country can import, which is often so in Latin America, an
increase in the rate of investment, even in public works with very
low import content, can produce inflationary pressure on the
economy, because the additional money that is made available
creates a demand for imports that cannot be satisfied. Increases in
private or public savings may tend to depress the level of economic
activity, because there is little chance of converting these savings
into investments that do not add to inflation. In these circumstances, to maintain investment rates that permit reasonable levels
of 'open employment', the Latin American countries have
frequently sought external financing. The problem has not been the
impossibility of increasing monetary savings, but rather the futility
of investing them if the economy does not generate the necessary
external resources to pay for an increase of imports.[1]

If Latin America were to achieve an increase in the rate of investment on the basis of a growth in external resources, it would
be able to make better use of its work force, many of whom are
under-employed or unemployed. This state of affairs is the
more deplorable since the labour that is being wasted in Latin
America is more capable of contributing towards higher rates of
economic growth than are the unemployed in other developing

Literacy Rates for Selected Latin American Countries
(1950 and estimates for 1970) (percentages of population)

	1950	1970
Argentina	86.4 (1947)	94.0
Trinidad & Tobago	73.9	93.0
Costa Rica	79.4	89.0
Mexico	55.9	73.0
Brazil	49.3	71.0
Peru	47.0	71.0
Venezuela	51.0	70.0
Dominican Republic	42.9	70.0
El Salvador	38.4	58.0
Bolivia	32.1	47.0
Haiti	10.5	24.0
Latin America	52.1	73.0

Source: Organization of American States, *Analysis of the Economic and Social
Evolution of Latin America since the Inception of the Alliance for Progress*, CIES/1636 rev.
1 (Washington, D.C., 3 August 1971), p. 55.

regions. The capacity of Latin America's labour force is high thanks to the progress achieved in education; in countries such as Argentina, Chile, and Uruguay the standard has been high since as long ago as the end of the last century, and in others more recently. The literacy rates are indicative of this; they still show some disparities among the individual countries of Latin America, but there have been enormous advances in the past 20 years.

Even in the poorest countries, progress in education has not been confined merely to acquiring literacy. Enrolment in secondary and higher education has grown at a faster rate than in primary education in the past decade. Also, more emphasis has been put on technical training for industry, agriculture, and business, through apprenticeship courses, on-the-job training, and traditional education systems.

Despite these achievements, to ensure that enough people acquire knowledge and skills equal to the tasks of development, education should be further expanded and its quality and relevance improved. Until the proportion of pupils completing the elementary school curriculum is raised from its present level of 30 per cent, there will be too few candidates for secondary and higher education. At the same time primary education needs to provide a more solid grounding in basic subjects than it has done up to now. Secondary education should be geared less to cramming students with useless knowledge in a nineteenth-century European fashion, and more to developing their aptitudes and offering sound technical and vocational training.

The Latin American countries should pay particular attention to higher education. Most countries are deficient in engineers and technicians, and need to educate more people in these subjects. What they lack most, however, are well-trained managers, both in public administration and in the productive sectors. The problem, in this instance, is rather that, because university teaching is badly oriented, graduates in political science, history, or classics do not make good managers and administrators, as they do in the industrialized countries. That Latin America is not making the best use of its professionals, who are educated at great expense, is evident from the proportion of the region's professionals and technicians who are working in industry, which is much lower than in the industrialized countries.

The acute shortage of suitably qualified people in industry is one aspect of what is perhaps the fundamental weakness of the economic policy of the post-war period. This is the failure of the Latin American countries to attach sufficient importance to developing a capability to absorb technology. Industry has made little

Proportion of all Professionals and Technicians Employed in Manufacturing Industries 1960

Country	percentage
Argentina	9.1
Brazil	7.6
Chile	8.3
Colombia[a]	11.9
United States	23.0
Norway	16.0
Netherlands	17.9

[a] *datum refers to 1963*

Source: Mariano Ramírez and Elvidio Parra, *Profesionales y Técnicos en América Latina* (Washington D.C.: Organization of American States, June 1968), p. 17. Data from OECD publications.

progress in adapting imported technology to Latin American conditions, and even less in inventing new techniques in fields and processes of special interest to the region. The problem stems not from the feasibility of doing so, but from an industrial structure and organization that has prevented Latin America from generating the kind of scientific and technological capacity that countries such as Italy, Czechoslovakia, or Japan managed to achieve at a stage of economic development when their *per capita* income was still lower than that of Argentina, Venezuela, Mexico, or the southeast of Brazil today. Discussion of the problem is further confused by an almost obsessive belief that Latin Americans are unable to cope with technical concepts.

Latin America should take special notice of the policies pursued by the most recent arrivals on the scene of modern technology, such as Japan, Israel, and a few of the socialist countries. Their example of concentrating scarce research resources in developing techniques suited to their particular circumstances could be emulated to great advantage by the Latin American countries. Cases in point are the processing of tropical fruits for international markets, the extraction and processing of heavy petroleum in Venezuela, food technology in Argentina, where research has been undertaken but has not been thorough enough, and the utilization of limited water resources in Mexico.

Latin America has also neglected to develop the managerial competence that is required for a proper use of technology. Policies should aim at furnishing training and information services that enable managers to choose among the alternative technologies available. Management techniques are equally important in determining the adaptation and organizational layout of production processes.

Though in recent years there has been much concern about the problems of technology in Latin America, the most relevant aspects have been ignored and attention has been focussed on two side issues : the cost of technology and the need to develop more labour-intensive methods. In fact, the cost of technology need not be high, and its application can assist the creation of more employment, provided that growth is stepped up and sensible economic policies followed.

The contention that Latin America ought to develop 'suitable' technology that uses more manpower in industry overlooks the existence of so-called intermediate technology. This encompasses production techniques that the industrialized countries have discarded because of the sharp rise in labour costs, but many of which Latin America could easily use to its economic advantage. Particularly apt cases would be those where the introduction of labour-saving capital equipment has not been accompanied by an improvement in the type or quality of the product.

Even in production processes where technology is most advanced and most subject to change, such as electronics or even iron and steel, there is great scope for varying the organization of the factors of production. Possibilities for employing manpower exist not only in the use of more labour-intensive machinery and methods (a typical case of which can be found in the clothing industry), but also to a still greater extent in auxiliary production processes such as packing, assembly, supplying inputs to the factory, and the process of interfusing the various phases of production. At the same time, industry requires a whole range of services directly related to the production process. The amount of employment generated by investment in industry is much greater than is commonly supposed, and is not necessarily diminished by the adoption of modern technology.

In the past 20 years, employment in industry has been growing at about the same rate as the work force and sometimes faster, as in Mexico. Moreover, since the percentage of the work force in industry in Mexico is still low compared with a country such as Argentina, it will probably grow very rapidly as Mexico develops. Furthermore, the expansion of industry seems to have created throughout the region a large number of new jobs in higher productivity services associated with industrialization.

In Latin America as a whole, open unemployment is currently at about 10 per cent of the work force. This problem has naturally long been one of the principal policy concerns of government

officials and politicians, who are obliged to respond to the heavy
pressure of public opinion. Recently, however, unemployment and
under-employment have come to be regarded as a cause rather
than a symptom of inadequate development. This view is mistaken; lack of development causes unemployment, which should
be tackled by increasing growth. In Brazil, where recent policy has
been successfully directed to maximizing production and growth,
during the period 1968–70 jobs were created at the rate of 675,000
a year, compared with an increase in the work force of only
500,000 a year, while the hours worked by each person increased.
As a result unemployment and under-employment have decreased
and wages have risen.

Brazil: Overall Trend of Employment, 1968–70 (thousands of workers)

	1968[a] (A)	1970[a] (B)	Change (B–A)
Work force [b]	29,292	30,295	1,003
Employment [b]	28,222	29,570	1,348
Agricultural	12,181	12,496	315
Non-agricultural	16,041	17,074	1,033
Employment by working hours per week			
Agricultural	12,181	12,496	315
Less than 40 hours	2,258	2,078	– 180
40 hours and more	9,365	10,019	654
Temporarily absent	558[c])	399	– 159
Non-Agricultural	16,041	17,074	1,033
Less than 40 hours	3,181	2,596	– 585
40 hours and more	11,610	13,317	1,707
Temporarily absent	1,250[c])	1,161	– 89

(a) Situation in the first quarter of each year.
(b) Population aged 14 years and over.
(c) Includes 'unknown'.

Source: Secretariat of the Inter-American Committee on the Alliance for
Progress, *Domestic Efforts and the Needs for External Financing for the Development of
Brazil*, CIAP 1553 (Washington, 6 June 1972).

To propose that the creation of employment ought to be the
central objective of the economic development process, is to miss
the point of the issue.[2] The fundamental objective of social welfare,
around which the debate revolves, is improved consumption, yet
Latin America cannot increase its consumption unless it produces
more. It is nevertheless true that a policy of maximizing production
for both internal and external markets may not immediately
achieve full employment, because of structural rigidities such as

an inadequately capacitated work force; in these circumstances, the problem of distributing incomes so as to increase consumption could be solved by means other than the creation of unproductive jobs. Indeed, governments should take firm and effective action to enable the poorest groups to obtain a fairer share of the national wealth. Such action must include family planning services and programmes for cheap housing, education, and technical training. The resources redistributed in this way must come, however, from a reduction in the consumption of the higher income groups and not from public or private savings; otherwise growth is stifled, as it has been in many instances.

Income is certainly not likely to be redistributed by the artificial creation of employment which increases production costs and prices, consequently lowering real wages. Policies aimed at distributing income more fairly will have a better chance of succeeding if there is more income available for distribution.

II. ECONOMIC POLICY AND PLANNING

To make full use of their potential, the Latin American countries will need thoroughly to revise the economic policies that have been undermined and overladen by post-war development strategy. The organization of the production system needs to be decentralized, so as to facilitate the process of decision-making, and to allocate the region's human and financial resources to the highest priorities. Greater pragmatism is required in both the public and private sectors; the administrative skills at Latin America's disposal should be concentrated on running the economy so as to ensure that essential policies are implemented as effectively as possible.

The rapid and apparently solid results of post-war development strategy have concealed the need for more coherent overall economic policies. They have appeared to vindicate the belief, which was even construed in theoretical terms, that in Latin America's circumstances 'imbalance', whether in the form of fiscal deficits, inflation, or industrialization at all costs, was the best means of inducing economic growth. Largely because of facile results and a conviction of the virtues of 'imbalance', overall economic policies have been only superficially planned and applied.

In the early 1960s, Latin America became the battlefield for a sterile debate between 'monetarists' and 'structuralists', on the causes and cures of inflation.[3] Only recently, when inflation became a serious problem in the industrialized countries, did it occur to the 'monetarists' that social pressures had much to do with rising prices, and that, to be effective, monetary and fiscal measures to combat inflation had to be accompanied by incomes policies and other social measures.

The 'structuralists', for their part, identified external bottlenecks and inadequate agricultural production as the main causes of inflation, and concluded that planning would obviate both by achieving a balanced growth of supply. However, in conceiving how planning should function in the mixed economies of Latin America, they overstressed the importance of handling real variables, and neglected the need for fiscal, balance-of-payments, and monetary policies that would create the conditions necessary for planning to succeed.

Many of the inconsistencies in economic management can be traced directly to the fact that no clear-cut distinction has been made between planning and the conduct of economic policy, which have not always advanced side by side. In Latin America, both planning and economic policy have important roles to play, and it is most expedient for them to be fully co-ordinated at all levels.

In the mixed economies of Latin America planning can achieve little if economic policy does not establish an adequate and stable general framework for the most efficient combination of the factors of production. Growth can take place and can even be stimulated in conditions of imbalance and instability; indeed, it has been, but in the long run the achievements are defeated by inflation, which makes it difficult to plan the expansion of production both at the national and at the company level. The conditions of unstable prices that have prevailed in many Latin American countries since the war, have discouraged long-term investment planning decisions, because, with an uncertain future, rapid returns were considered more important. In many instances, inflation has also weakened local entrepreneurs, who are usually less able than foreign enterprises to finance prolonged periods of liquidity shortages. Furthermore, since in a situation of chronic inflation, prices and incomes almost always overtake public revenues, the administrative functions of the state are seriously affected.

Long periods of wide discrepancies between nominal and real interest rates in the money and capital markets have been frequent in Latin America. These discrepancies tend to stimulate speculation rather than to allocate resources to productive activities. Overvalued currencies can spur internal activity by shielding national markets, but they seriously hamper exports of manufactures. In several Latin American countries, periods of overvalued and unstable domestic currency have sharply affected export incentives, and have forced or justified the application of high tariff duties or quantitative restrictions to limit imports – a situation that has helped to perpetuate the inward-looking growth model.

Strains have been placed on economic policy-making by a development model that did not rationalize protection and allowed inflation to get out of hand. Whether it is induced by the pull of demand or the push of costs, inflation is difficult to decelerate. Harder still is to rationalize industrial production once trade union, political, and entrepreneurial interests are vested in inefficient industries.

There is by no means a single formula or a ready-made programme of fiscal, monetary, and exchange-rate policies to cope with these problems. Such policies have to be adapted to the conditions prevailing in each country, and adjusted as these conditions, external and internal, change. The advantages and disadvantages of a particular programme differ according to circumstances, but the important point is that they cannot be established solely on the needs of the moment, but must be a function of general economic strategy.

Such programmes cannot succeed for more than the short run unless they ensure an adequate growth in exports, especially manufactures, which must be stimulated by means of a co-ordinated policy effort, comprising exchange-rate management, financial assistance, technical assistance, and tax concessions, the organizing of marketing channels and facilities in foreign countries, export credits, and tariff reductions, wherever they can be negotiated.

General policies, however well conceived and managed, cannot alone ensure that the objectives of a new development strategy will be attained. Detailed planning at a practical level also has a major role. Planning commissions were set up in most Latin American countries at about the time that the Alliance for Progress programme was launched. The planning commissions themselves have had a positive effect in the co-ordinating and rationalizing of economic decision-making, especially in those countries where they have been placed directly under the authority of the chief executive. Also, some of the proposals for structural reform contained in the plans have been influential, such as the land tenure and tax reforms undertaken in Latin America during the 1960s.

However, the plans produced in the past decade have largely been intellectual exercises, confined to abstract generalizations. A perusal of these plans leaves something of an impression that all items had equal priority, so that none emerged as the key factor. The main function of the plans has been to present projections of internal economic and social variables, demonstrating the size of the external gap and hence the need for external financing. The plans have been turned to this purpose to such an extent that, though they are supposedly guides to action, many of them have been prepared during the period for which they were intended to be regulating the economy.

Planning has thus had very little impact on economic behaviour, since it has been concerned with these esoteric projections and has not been co-ordinated at the administrative level to act as the kind of medium- and long-term guide to economic policy that can contribute to key decisions, such as the allocation of public investment and the influencing of private investment.

In general terms, planning should give much greater heed to prospective elements of development than it has done up to now. This would mean, for example, a thorough analysis of the role of petroleum in Venezuela, the modernization of industry in Argentina, and, in the case of Mexico, the need to offset the necessary expansion of economic relations with the United States by more active participation in the economic integration of Latin America.

Planning should also perform an important role in fields where decisions are not governed by market forces nor by stimuli provided by general economic policy. This is the case with basic industries, which require large outlays of capital and modern technology, in many instances must of necessity be monopolies, and depend on exports to be able to produce on an efficient scale. Governments are closely involved in such investments, either through the granting of permits, accepting the participation of foreign private investment, undertaking the investment itself, or taking a share in mixed-capital ventures.

Similarly in most Latin American countries the preparation and execution of multi-annual investment budgets for the bulk of public investment should be subject to direct planning, so as to ensure consistency and continuity in the execution of the more important projects. The development and management of state enterprises is another field which has not received proper consideration in the planning process, despite the significant proportion of g.d.p. now generated by these enterprises in most countries of the region.

Much could be accomplished by the application of planning to technology and the environment. Contrary to common belief, Latin America is better placed than the developed countries to adopt the latest technologies in many industries, especially in those that have not been widely established in the region and are not inhibited by large existing investments or strong vested interests. In particular, Latin American industries could from the outset concentrate on new technologies that cause a minimum of pollution, whereas the same industries in the developed countries need to spend large sums on adapting older technologies so as to reduce pollution. Latin America could, for example, gain some advance on the industrialized countries by beginning now to produce motor vehicles causing very little pollution. This would both help to improve the environment and open up sizeable export markets.

As regards another aspect of the environment, Latin America should guard against the tendency to import patterns of urban development from the industrialized nations. Latin American countries are already allowing their cities to sprawl in a way that imitates, or even exaggerates, all the negative features of urban growth in the industrialized world. Unless the Latin Americans learn from the mistakes of others, by carefully planning their urban development, they will be confronted with the same environmental problems that the industrialized countries are now facing. For example, there has been no attempt to design cities with modern and efficient public transport systems, where the use of private cars would be severely curtailed. Not only would such principles benefit the environment, but they would also involve less expenditure than does the expansion of the infrastructure required by an unrestricted increase in the number of cars.

III. THE EXTERNAL SECTOR AND REGIONAL POLICY

The inward-looking development strategy adopted in Latin America during the post-war period has created a situation of external dependence that is imputed to every cause except the strategy itself, for which Latin American policy-makers of all ideological tendencies should be held responsible.

The share of the Latin American countries in world trade has decreased to levels well below those reached by industrialized nations with an overall demand comparable to that of the larger countries of the region. This has made it impossible to use existing resources efficiently by specializing in certain types of production, as Sweden, Italy, and Australia, for instance, have done. Furthermore, the slow growth of exports has deprived Latin America of external resources to pay for the imports that it needs and for the services associated with technology, management, and foreign private investment in general.

This fact is widely recognized in recent literature, which stresses the need to increase exports for faster economic growth and more employment.[4] In *Change and Development* it is suggested that ex-

Ratio of Imports and Exports to GDP for Selected Countries, 1969
(percentages)

	Exports	Imports
Argentina	7.0	6.9
Brazil	5.8	6.7
Mexico	4.8	6.9
Australia	14.0	15.1
Belgium	44.0	43.7
Italy	14.2	15.1
New Zealand	22.4	18.6
Spain	15.1	14.5
Sweden	19.4	20.2

Source: Based on United Nations, *Yearbook of National Accounts Statistics 1969*; Supplement to International Financial Statistics, 1972.

ports could be increased by extending import substitution to a regional framework. The implicit assertion is that for economic reasons alone it is necessary to expand trade within the region. This is certainly true, and it follows that a re-examination of the state of economic integration in Latin America should be directed not towards over-ambitious and utopian concepts, but towards pragmatic action that will facilitate the acceleration of trade within the region in the coming years.

The Montevideo Treaty laid down a programme of liberalization for intra-regional trade that would eventually embrace all Latin American countries, including those of the Central American Common Market. Negotiations made a promising start but continued more slowly as time went on, until at the tenth meeting of the contracting parties in Caracas in 1970 negotiations appeared to come to a halt.

This slowing-down is not, as is sometimes thought in Latin America, due to the lack of a more imaginative framework for integration which, like the Cartagena Agreement, would attempt to plan the whole process of economic integration. Ambitious schemes for integrating economic and social policy are unlikely to flourish as long as the flow of trade within Latin America is too slender to establish a basic community of interests. The experience and success of the European Economic Community shows that the most effective way to achieve integration is by the freeing of trade. One need only imagine at what stage the EEC would be today if it had attempted to integrate in advance its regional investments, fiscal regulations, social legislation, exchange systems, and monetary policy.

It is not because the Montevideo Treaty was largely confined to trade liberalization that LAFTA has begun to falter, but because the concessions have been negotiated by procedures that are too complicated, and because they exclude many products – especially manufactures already being produced in the region – in which intra-regional trade could have expanded faster. Another impediment to progress lay in the various economic and political setbacks suffered by Argentina and Brazil during the 1960s. In Latin America, much more than in Europe, industrial capacity varies according to economic size; these two countries between them account for more than half of LAFTA trade, so that any deterioration in their trade seriously affects the whole region. Furthermore, at no stage did the larger countries consider giving significant preferential treatment to the smaller countries, despite the obvious advantages that they possess because of their higher level of industrial development.

In Latin America measures to promote integration should give more attention to the comparative advantages of the larger countries with their more advanced industries. To dispel the fear that regional integration exposes the smaller national economies to the dangers of unfair competition, the larger countries should take a more decided initiative in giving preferences to their weaker neighbours. It is also important that institutions such as the Inter-American Development Bank, the Andean Development Corporation, and the Central American Bank for Economic Integration should assume responsibility for programming and financing integration projects for particular industries in specific groups of countries. In these undertakings both the Latin American Integration Fund and the Latin American Industrial Modernization Fund could play a major role.[5]

Speeding up the economic integration of Latin America is not only necessary from an economic point of view, but also indispensable to strengthen Latin America's unity in its relations with the industrialized countries. The region urgently needs to broaden and diversify its economic relations with the industrialized nations, and to participate more fully in the world economy.

To this end, Latin America should seek to handle international financial transactions in ways best suited to the new patterns of economic power among the industrialized countries, and to establish relationships on foreign direct investment, whether from capitalist sources or state enterprises in socialist countries, of a kind that benefits both parties. Latin America also needs to act constructively on trade in traditional exports, whose importance has sometimes been underestimated; the market for some primary commodities has been expanding and may expand even more rapidly in the next twenty-five years. At the same time, Latin America should attempt to set up new forms of trade in manufactures that are advantageous both to the industrialized countries and to the region itself.

The current discussion of new international economic and monetary arrangements offers Latin America an opportunity to attain these goals; the region should analyse its situation and present well-reasoned and negotiable arguments that will compel the attention of the industrialized countries.

NOTES

[1] For a fuller treatment of this point, see Felipe Pazos, 'El Financiamiento, externo de la América Latina: aumento progresivo o disminución gradual' in *El Trimestre Económico*, April/June 1971.

[2] See Irving Beller, 'Latin America's Unemployment Problem' in *Monthly Labor Review*, XCIII (November 1970), pp. 3–10.

[3] Perhaps the best contemporary judgement of this situation was that of Sir Arthur Lewis: 'All one can safely say is that in a number of Latin American countries the government gets away with printing money to an extent which is puzzling to visitors from any other continent, and one cannot help feeling that the people deserve better governments than they get'. Werner Baer and Isaac Kerstenetzky, eds., *Inflation and Growth in Latin America* (New Haven: Yale University Press, 1964), p. 24.

[4] See Raúl Prebisch, *Change and Development: Latin America's Great Task* (Washington, D.C.: Inter-American Development Bank, 1970), and *Towards Full Employment. A Programme for Colombia* (Geneva: International Labour Office, 1970).

[5] See below, Chapter 10.

PART THREE

Partnership with the Industrialized Countries

Chapter 7

New Bearings in the
Inter-American System

LATIN AMERICA'S RELATIONS with the United States are at present in a state of flux, and will probably change rapidly during the next few years. A radical shift in the position of the United States in the world economy has coincided with dissatisfaction in both the Americas at the limitations and constraints of the economic framework that has grown up under the inter-American system.

The United States government has been deeply engrossed in the disruption of the Bretton Woods monetary system. Matters came to a head in 1971 when the position of the dollar balances held in the rest of the world was weakened by the first adverse trade balance recorded by the United States in the twentieth century. This state of affairs outweighs all other considerations in United States economic policy; the need to expand exports requires the control of inflation at home and the negotiation of more liberal trade agreements with Europe, Japan, and the other industrialized countries. There is also concern about short-term capital movements. The rapid flow of massive funds across national boundaries can cause minor instability to develop into a major international problem.

For these and other reasons there has been a waning of enthusiasm for the type of co-operation envisaged in the programme of the Alliance for Progress. The United States government has come to realize that the institutional framework set up to promote co-operation has now become largely ineffectual, while the Latin Americans have reached the conclusion that in many instances their interests diverge from those of the United States and would benefit from a broadening of the region's external relations to include the other industrialized countries.

The inter-American system is now in a state of transition that is frustrating for both the United States and Latin America. Response to the evident need for change takes two forms, neither of which is altogether appropriate. Within the system efforts are being made to broaden its scope; the European countries and Japan are to become subscribing members of the Inter-American Development Bank and hope to be observers in the Organization of American States, as Canada already is. The other view, held mainly outside these institutions, is that the system has lost its *raison d'être* and should disappear, perhaps to be replaced by a two-tier arrangement that would provide for an inner group comprising all the Latin American countries, and an outer group including the United States and other industrialized countries.

Western Europe, Japan, and the socialist countries tend to consider the inter-American arrangements between the Latin American countries and the United States as too narrow. In their present form, the inter-American institutions are not appropriate means to expand Latin America's ties with the industrialized countries. On the other hand, Latin America would be foolish to break well-established and valuable institutional links. The United States and Latin America should seek a middle course that would benefit them both.

I. FROM A HIGH CALLING TO A LOW PROFILE

The late 1950s produced a convergence of events that disposed the United States and the Latin American countries to draw up the programme of the Alliance for Progress, under which large amounts of external finance were to be transferred from the United States to Latin America during the 1960s. The achievements of the programme were less than expected, and by the end of the decade there was disenchantment with the Alliance on both sides.

For some years after the Second World War, both government policy and public attitudes in the United States towards Latin America were conditioned by a concept of national self-interest emerging from the Cold War. It was widely believed that the United States was confronted by a monolithic communist system bent on world domination and was responsible for containing it, wherever it might seek to expand; to this end, various geographical alliances were formed and foreign aid was granted. Since, in the early post-war years, policy-makers considered Latin America less patently threatened by the Cold War than other areas, they paid it relatively little attention.

Meanwhile ECLA was propagating in Latin America an economic thesis stressing the material need and the moral justification for temporary transfers of resources from the developed countries to Latin America, to compensate for the losses suffered through the deterioration in the region's terms of trade. These temporary flows of financial resources, it was held, would supplement internal savings and be the leaven needed to activate a process of accelerated and self-sustained growth.

By the late 1950s Latin American governments had accumulated large amounts of short- and medium-term external debt. The populist governments in power in Argentina and Brazil, which were committed to 'instantaneous development' programmes, subscribed to the ECLA ideology as it had been set out in a meeting of Latin American leaders at Quitandinha in 1954. They began to press the United States for aid by various means, such as the 'Operação Pan Americana' instigated by the President of Brazil, Juscelino Kubitschek. To make a better case for aid, some Latin Americans also indiscriminately cultivated an image of their continent as one of poverty, under-development, and social inequalities.

It was against this background that Fidel Castro's success in bringing about a communist revolution in Cuba with a great deal of popular support convinced Washington that Latin America was after all a Cold War theatre. The general, though imprecise, conception of Latin America as backward and underprivileged, and the expectation of an imminent repetition of Castro's feat elsewhere in Latin America led to the changes of opinion in the United States that determined policy through most of the 1960s. The first manifestation of this revised policy was a commitment of $500 million for social development projects, made at Bogotá in 1960, which was followed in 1961 by the programme of the Alliance for Progress, launched at Punta del Este.

At the institutional level, several organizations were set up within the Organization of American States to co-ordinate Alliance policy jointly with the Inter-American Development Bank. The bank had been established in 1959 as a regional institution with a membership of 21 Latin American countries and the United States. It had been conceived as a vehicle for the multilateral management of funds originating mostly in the United States that would contribute to the economic and social progress of Latin America.

The Inter-American Economic and Social Council (CIES), and its subsidiary bodies, operating within the Organization of American States, were responsible for the multilateral political aspects of the Alliance. One of the functions of the Council was to evaluate or assist in the formulation of national development plans, so as to ensure that they could be supported by adequate external financing. This role was first delegated to the so-called Panel of

Experts, and later transferred to the Inter-American Committee on the Alliance for Progress (CIAP), created in 1963.

Both in the United States and in many Latin American circles, the Alliance for Progress aroused high hopes that steady advances would be achieved by co-operation between democratic, reform-minded, Latin American governments and Washington. United States policy-makers thought that their country could provide the essential stimulus and the requisite financial and technical assistance to enable the Latin American countries to introduce social reforms, economic planning, and increased savings and investment, and so reach a stage where steady self-sustaining growth would be possible and Latin America could fend for itself.

The Alliance did bring about better understanding between the United States and Latin America, basically through changes in United States attitudes towards Latin American development problems. In a fairly short time United States policy-makers came to accept what ECLA had been propounding; it was acknowledged that the region needed to obtain long-term public funds, to modernize its tax systems and reform much of its land tenure. Even regional economic integration, which had formerly been opposed, was recognized as desirable.

In the United States the Alliance for Progress was viewed as the Latin American equivalent of the Marshall Plan in post-war Europe. There were, however, important differences between the two; the European countries responded to the offer of assistance from the United States by setting up the Organization for European Economic Co-operation, through which they administered the programme, albeit under the close scrutiny of Washington. Under the Marshall Plan, efforts were concentrated on restoring and increasing basic industrial and agricultural production and creating financial stability; the success of these efforts made it possible for Europe to pass from bilateral to multilateral trading in the mid-1950s.

The assumptions and methods of the Alliance for Progress programme laid similar emphasis on the use of external finance for a short period to help Latin American countries to reach a stage where they could achieve self-sustained growth. Under the Alliance, however, unlike under the Marshall Plan, the United States government was directly involved in administering the programme; the allocation of the greater part of the funds was determined bilaterally between the United States and individual Latin American governments, rather than through the multilateral channels of the inter-American system, which could have performed co-ordinating and administrative functions similar to those of the OEEC.

Though the United States government and the Inter-American institutions insisted that the Latin American countries make corresponding internal efforts in the shape of, for example, revising their tax systems, carrying out land reform, and extending public health facilities, the programme did not sufficiently stress the need to use the funds to expand and improve production. Nor did it give enough weight to increasing exports, which was essential if the temporary flow of external resources was to have the desired result.

The neglect of trade has reinforced the tendency of the balance of payments on current account between the United States and Latin America to move persistently against Latin America.[1] The overall payments position has, however, remained more or less in balance because the large transfers of net public sector capital received by Latin America from the United States in the form of 'aid' have largely offset the region's current account deficit with the United States. Only in certain years, such as 1968, has Latin America had to use its trade surpluses with Europe and Japan to cover the deficit.

Public medium- and long-term financing authorized by the United States for Latin America between 1961 and 1970 amounted to over $11,000 million; this figure includes Export-Import Bank loans, which are the United States equivalent of European and Japanese export credits, and account for over $2,000 million. The Inter-American Development Bank has also

Authorizations of Official External Economic Development Financing for Latin America, 1961 to 1970 (selected US Fiscal Years)
($ million)

	1961	1966	1970	10-year Total
AID, Food for Peace, Peace Corps, other	477	810	538	6,487
Contributions to IDB (including Social Progress Trust Fund)	80	274	303	2,485
SUB-TOTAL	557	1,084	841	8,972
Export-Import Bank long-term loans (5 years or more)	450	128	183	2,191
TOTAL	1,007	1,212	1,024	11,163

Source: US AID.

been able to place over $1,500 million in bonds in European markets with the backing of the uncalled portion of the United States capital in the bank. Authorizations of United States bilateral aid showed a marked decrease in 1969 and 1970, but the total amount in those years was still roughly equivalent to the average annual allocation for the decade.

A large part of Latin America's deficit on current account is attributable to the fact that net outward service payments for transport, patents and royalties, and above all investment income, have more than doubled in ten years. All the same, had Latin America's exports to the United States grown more rapidly, the deficit would now be a much more manageable problem. In fact, Latin America's exports to the United States grew only slowly over the decade, and the region's share of the United States market fell significantly, while imports into Latin America from the United States continued to grow at a rate that kept the United States share consistently high (43 per cent in 1968 compared with 45 per cent in 1960); this was to some extent because a large proportion of 'aid' was granted on condition that it be spent in the United States. As a result the trade balance, which during the Second World War was decidedly favourable for Latin America, and in 1950–52 still showed about $200 million in the region's favour, became increasingly adverse for Latin America, especially if Venezuela, with her trade surplus from oil exports, is excluded.

Latin American Trade Balance with the United States,
excluding Venezuela ($ million)

Year	Exports	Imports	Balance
1962	2,327.9	2,936.9	− 609.0
1964	2,454.8	3,228.6	− 773.8
1968	3,023.0	3,961.0	− 938.0
1970	3,271.7	4,993.6	− 1,721.9

IMF, *Direction of Trade.*

The poor performance of Latin America's exports to the United States is explained partly by the region's failure to pay attention to changes in United States import requirements, and partly by United States commercial policies towards Latin America. The pattern of United States import demand has concentrated more on manufactures and less on primary products, which in many cases have been replaced by substitutes; unfortunately the range of Latin American export goods is narrow, and heavily concentrated in the primary products. The demand for tropical food products is growing very slowly in the United States and some consumption patterns are changing; the *per capita* consumption of coffee, for example, is gradually declining. The demand for metals is in general growing more satisfactorily, but they are subject to wide price fluctuations. In the whole range of primary commodities of major importance Latin America faces competition in the United States market from producers in other continents, and in the case of temperate foodstuffs and certain raw materials must also compete against domestic production, in some instances heavily protected. Latin America, except for Colombia, Brazil, and Mexico in recent years, has not exploited the opportunities offered by the United States in the past 25 years as a market for manufactures. Spain, Yugoslavia, and many developing countries of South-East Asia, as well as the industrialized countries, have taken advantage of this, but Latin America has hardly done so, though for many reasons the United States should be a natural market for Latin American products.

On the other hand, United States commercial policy towards Latin America has not been fully in accordance with the spirit of co-operation that supposedly reigns between the two regions. Restrictions on traditional products have been maintained, and in a few cases augmented, and several policies have been introduced that discriminate against Latin American products. Quantitative restrictions are imposed by the United States on agricultural products such as cotton, meat, and dairy products. In addition, meat, fruit, vegetables, and processed foods are subject to a variety of quality, packaging, health and sanitary standards that are frequently used for justifying barriers to imports. There are also seasonal tariffs, which in particular affect Mexico, Central America, the Caribbean, and countries of the South that are capable of satisfying United States demand for out-of-season temperate agricultural products. The abolition of restrictions on overland shipments of petroleum to the United States has favoured Canada, who in fact resells Venezuelan petroleum on the American market. In recent years Brazilian efforts to stimulate sales of soluble coffee in the United States met strong resistance when Brazilian sales affected United States makers of the product, who import coffee beans from Africa. Colombia has also been experiencing difficulties and restrictions in exports of manufactures such as textiles.

The Alliance for Progress programme achieved some success in improving Latin America's relations with the United States. The Inter-American Committee on the Alliance for Progress (CIAP) has had a favourable influence. It has prepared informative annual reviews of the economic situation in each country of the region, containing recommendations that have later been quoted in providing bilateral financial co-operation. The Fulbright Amendment to the Foreign Assistance Act of 1966 makes a recommendation of CIAP mandatory in authorizing loans to individual countries under the Alliance for Progress. On the basis of this amendment, the Committee has also rejected the imposition by Washington of certain political conditions on bilateral assistance.

By the mid-1960s the goal of a *per capita* income growth rate of 2.5 per cent, set in the Charter of Punta del Este, was being met by most Latin American countries, and advances had been made in raising standards of education, housing, and health. Nevertheless, there were profound and persistent doubts on the validity of such a programme, both in Latin America and in the United States. Some Latin American governments that benefited from Alliance funds wished to attribute its success to themselves rather than to the joint programme; this bias was accentuated by the opposition, voiced by groups ranging from centre-left to left-wing asserting that the Alliance was at best paternalist and at worst a tool for the infiltration of 'yankee imperialism'. The fear of United States interventionism was rekindled in 1965 when the United States government, uncertain of obtaining a prompt favourable response from the Organization of American States, took unilateral action in the Dominican Republic, as it had done in Guatemala in 1954 and in Cuba in 1960–61.

In the United States, Washington's policies in general came to be more and more seriously questioned, chiefly as a result of the Vietnam War, domestic social problems, and economic problems both inside the country and abroad. In the event, communism in Cuba proved not to be the danger to the United States that had been forecast in 1960 and seemed to be confirmed by the 'missile crisis'. United States policy underwent a reappraisal that eventually led to new approaches, such as President Nixon's visit to China. United States policy-makers began to appreciate that the aspirations of the Alliance for Progress had been unrealistic, and that 'aid' could have only limited influence on the course of events in Latin American countries.[2]

II. THE FUTURE OF RELATIONS BETWEEN LATIN AMERICA AND THE UNITED STATES

The first moves towards modifying the framework of economic relations set up under the inter-American system were made by the Latin American governments. A new role was assigned to the

Special Committee for Latin American Co-ordination (CECLA), which had been created by the Inter-American Economic and Social Council in 1963 to co-ordinate the positions of the Latin American members of the Organization of American States on economic issues that were to be discussed at the first meeting of UNCTAD[3]. The Committee continued to perform a useful, though little noticed, function as an informal body for co-ordinating trade policy until, in May 1969, it acquired new prominence by drawing up the Consensus of Viña del Mar. This document announced a joint Latin American position regarding economic co-operation between Latin America and the United States. It was virtually the first document of its kind to stress the importance of trade rather than aid, and to draw attention to barriers against trade in manufactured and semi-manufactured goods as distinct from those restricting primary products. The vigorous new role of CECLA in these matters was an important step in equipping Latin America with the means for concerted and effective action in its economic relations with the industrialized countries. CECLA has been responsible since 1969 for much of the activity in economic affairs in the OAS, and it was also the prime mover in the establishment of the Special Committee for Consultation and Negotiation (CECON).

The creation of CECON, which is a permanent body for negotiating trade and other commercial matters between Latin America and the United States, amounted to a major structural innovation in the inter-American system. It underlined a common position of the Latin American countries, and the need for new forms of inter-American co-operation in the economic and social field. Unlike earlier instruments of the inter-American system, CECON was intended from the start to provide a vehicle for bargaining between the United States and Latin America as a bloc, and hence on more equal terms. In this respect, CECON signifies

> the partial displacement of inter-American relations by essentially United States-Latin American relations. Thus, CECON reflects a reality: the divergent interests of the US and the Latin American countries on certain fundamental issues of trade and international finance.[4]

The initiatives taken by Latin America have been welcomed by the United States as an opportunity for redefining relations with Latin America.[5] The activist style of the Alliance for Progress has been discarded. It is now better understood that United States aid combined with direct efforts to influence the behaviour of

D

Latin American countries can create considerable tensions, and that the benefits are too often marginal and short-lived. The fundamental change that has taken place in United States policy can be appreciated by comparing extracts from speeches of two United States Presidents separated by eight years.

> Thus if the countries of Latin America are ready to do their part – and I am sure they are – then I believe the United States, for its part, should help provide resources of a scope and magnitude sufficient to make this bold development plan a success, just as we helped to provide, against nearly equal odds, the resources adequate to help rebuild the economies of Western Europe.
>
> (John F. Kennedy, White House address, 13 March 1961.)
>
> For years, we in the United States have pursued the illusion that we could remake continents. Conscious of our wealth and technology, seized by the force of our good intentions, driven by our habitual impatience, remembering the dramatic success of the Marshall Plan in post-war Europe, we have sometimes imagined that we knew what was best for everyone else and that we could and should make it happen.
>
> (Richard M. Nixon, 'Action for Progress in the Americas', an address given to the Inter-American Press Association, 31 October 1969.)

Inevitably the lower profile of the United States in Latin America has been interpreted as a diminution of Washington's interest. So far, its clearest expression has been a distinct shift away from bilateral aid granted by Washington to individual countries towards multilateral aid, channelled through the IDB and other international institutions. This change promises well for future relations, provided that it is accompanied by an expansion of trade. Unfortunately, the United States has so far responded only very cautiously to Latin American requests for the lowering of barriers to trade, especially in manufactured and semi-manufactured goods. This reluctance is partly caused by the general economic situation of the United States, which has both prompted protectionist tendencies and caused issues other than Latin America to loom much larger in the formulation of United States policy.

At present Latin America arouses little interest or concern among policy-makers in the United States. This was made very clear in August 1971 when Washington imposed a 10 per cent surcharge on all imports without making any concession to Latin America. It would have cost the United States very little to exempt Latin American goods from the surcharge; the excuse given by Washing-

ton for not doing so was that an exemption would have con-
travened GATT regulations, but if the desire to help Latin America
had been strong enough, no such regulation would have impeded
an appropriate decision.

The countries of Latin America should combine forces to im-
press on the United States that, in view of the region's propensity
to import United States products, and since the current account
balance is heavily adverse to Latin America because of debt
servicing and profit remittances, it would make sound economic
sense for the United States to co-operate by promoting a significant
increase in her imports from the region. In particular, Latin
America should drive home the point that any measure placing
restrictions on exports of manufactures to the United States is
especially damaging to Latin America because of its state of semi-
development. One suggestion that should be made is that, as
long as quotas are applied to United States imports of certain
industrial goods, Latin America should be given a proportionately
larger share than the industrialized countries in manufactures in
which it is trying to develop competitive advantages; for example,
in textiles and clothing.

It is to be expected that Latin America's efforts to increase its
exports of manufactured and semi-manufactured goods will meet
with numerous obstacles in the United States market. The
economic difficulties of the United States, particularly the country's
adverse trade balance and the effects of foreign competition on
domestic industry and employment, have encouraged a shift towards greater restriction, and away from freer trade. Trade unions
are abandoning their long-standing support of free trade; they are
challenging the trans-national corporations on the grounds that
they are 'exporting' jobs and so depriving workers in the United
States of employment. In the present conditions of unemployment
trade unions are unlikely to be convinced that, in the long run
and granted a prosperous economic situation in the United States,
workers both there and in Latin America could benefit from
liberalization; the first because they would be able to buy cheaper
goods, and the second because they would get better-paid jobs.

Even when the hoped-for improvement in the United States
economy is achieved and the impending changes in international
financial relations permit a return to normal trading, there still
may not be a swift reversal of protectionist leanings in the United
States. There are serious doubts over whether Washington will be
able to help effectively to expand and diversify Latin American
exports. Latin America needs to organize a competent and vigorous
lobby in the United States to promote its case. Such a lobby could

probably count on the backing of international corporations, which are interested in producing more cheaply, as well as the consumer groups, which are becoming increasingly influential.

There is overseas rising concern in the United States at the negative effects of private investment on the balance of payments. At the same time, Latin America's share of world-wide United States investment has been shrinking, largely because other regions, such as Europe, have become much more attractive. Even so, the book value of United States private direct investment, including reinvested profits, in Latin America increased by over $5,000 million in the last decade, so that by 1971 the total book value stood at more than $13,000 million.

In terms of cash flows, it is true that United States direct investment has had a negative impact on the overall Latin American balance of payments in the past decade. This has been caused mostly by profit remittances from Venezuela, and the fact that oil companies in that country have been disinvesting. If all other United States investments in Latin America are considered separately, net investment from the United States, which includes reinvested profits, would appear to be higher than the income derived from these investments.

Even so, the net balance in Latin America's favour is small, because the outflows represent returns on all United States direct investments in the region, made over many years, whereas the annual movement of new investment dollars to Latin America cannot be expected fully to compensate the returns on this accumulated total of assets. Private foreign investment should, however, be regarded in the broader context of the balance of payments as a whole, rather than as a simple and particular cash flow. From this point of view, if such investment made a bigger contribution to increasing export earnings, it would certainly abate what can be a very real concern for policy managers confronted by balance-of-payments difficulties, as is so often the case in Latin America.

For some time investment in mining has tended to be replaced by investment in manufacturing and services.[6] In Mexico, Brazil, and Argentina, between 60 and 70 per cent of United States investment is now in the manufacturing sector. This has usually meant a decline in the contribution of private foreign investment to export earnings because activity has switched from exporting minerals to producing manufactured goods for the domestic market. Lately, however, where conditions have been favourable, several United States firms established in Latin America, as well as some subsidiaries of large corporations, have begun to plan production for export, particularly within Latin America, but also to the United States. For example, under a special agreement between the governments many United States companies have set up so-called *maquila* industries in Mexico to manufacture products exclusively for export to the United States. These exports, which in 1966 were worth only $7 million, are today worth over $250 million. More recently, foreign companies in Brazil have started to produce goods for export to the United States.

Private direct United States investment will continue to be a troublesome point in relations between Latin America and the United States. However, given sounder development policies in Latin America, a greater willingness among private foreign investors to adapt themselves to new conditions, and a reasonably pragmatic approach on both sides, it should be possible to solve the problems that may arise. Perhaps the most delicate matter will be, as it is today, the question of take-overs of domestically owned firms. Indeed, this is such a sensitive area that it would be best if foreign investors avoided them. Latin American governments, for their part, should discourage them. In cases where it is considered beneficial for foreign investment to participate in the modernization of an existing industry, this should be done through joint ventures or other arrangements that avoid loss of national ownership.

Latin America and the United States will continue to be closely involved with each other because of their proximity and strong economic ties. Latin American nationalist attitudes and changing United States policy will probably lead to the placing of emphasis more on problems associated with economic relations (trade, foreign investment, transfers of technology, and finance), and less on internal development policies, which are the exclusive domain of the Latin American countries. President Nixon referred to this change of accent in his message to Congress on 18 February 1970 :

Too many of our development programmes were made for our neighbours instead of with them. This directive and tutorial style clashed with the growing self-assertiveness and nationalism of the other Western Hemisphere nations.

Furthermore, these relations will need to be conducted increasingly within the broader framework of Latin America's relations with the industrialized countries as a whole, and not merely within a closed inter-American system. To accommodate these new departures, the United States should carry out the Rockefeller Report's recommendation that Administration officials who handle relations with Latin America should be raised to a higher status.[7]

This will be particularly important for dealing with economic relations, which will be more complex when they are on a business rather than a charitable footing, and more closely concerned with trade and investment than they were during the 1960s. For the same reason, the organizations within the inter-American system that deal with economic matters should be remoulded.

Serious consideration should now be given to ways of supplying the external financial resources that Latin America will require during the coming decade to promote the internal changes needed to stimulate the region's international trade. Here again, the reconstruction of Europe provides an example, which was taken up at the meeting of the Heads of American States in Punta del Este in 1967.[8] Further consideration should now be given to providing development finance for the creation of two funds to accelerate economic integration and, with it, Latin American exports. A Latin American Integration Fund of $400 million, which could be capitalized in the course of a few years, would be mainly for financing the expansion of intra-Latin American trade. A Latin American Industrial Modernization Fund of $600 million, to be capitalized in the same way, could also make an enormous contribution to integration, the reduction of industrial costs, and the export of manufactures.

In line with the recent highly commendable trend towards multilateral development financing, both these funds should be placed under the Inter-American Development Bank or its subsidiary organs. Many of the region's needs for development finance can best be served by a regional bank handling international funds, as the IDB does, and the Bank should be strengthened in its development functions. The Bank should perhaps be transformed into a Latin American Investment Bank, and provision should also be made for the active participation in it of all the industrialized countries in accordance with the size of their trade with Latin America. (More will be said of this later.) Furthermore, as in the World Bank, a very clear distinction should be made between concessional finance operations and investment banking.

Given that the Alliance for Progress programme has to all intents and purposes come to an end, the bodies that were set up to conduct it should be thoroughly reappraised. It would be convenient for Latin America to maintain the Inter-American Economic and Social Council (CIES), which is already an important and well-established institutional link with the United States. The Inter-American Committee on the Alliance for Progress (CIAP), on the other hand, should admit the other industrialized countries as members, and play the more effective, though modest, role of a technical advisory body attached to a reorganized IDB to guide its aid allocations. A revision of this kind would provide a more flexible framework in which to solve problems between Latin America and the United States, and would allow Latin America to become a strong economic partner of the other industrialized countries. Such a development would be in the best interests of both the United States and Latin America.

NOTES

[1] The trend in the current account does not vary substantially if Venezuela is excluded, because this country's large trade surplus is counterbalanced almost entirely by the large remittances of the oil companies.

[2] For an analysis of the Alliance for Progress, see Jerome Levinson and Juan de Onís, *The Alliance that Lost its Way. A Critical Report on the Alliance for Progress* (Chicago: Quadrangle Books, for the Twentieth Century Fund, 1970).

[3] The idea of CECLA emerged during the preparation of a document presented to ECLA in December 1963 by a group of experts (Eduardo Figueroa, Plácido García Reynoso, Julio Lacarte, Carlos Lleras Restrepo, Jorge Sol, Marco do Reifo Monteiro, Enrique Gastón Valente, and Adalbert Krieger Vasena), who saw the need for a close co-ordination of Latin American trade policies and objectives for the region to make its requirements clear to the rest of the world.

[4] OAS, *Analysis of the Economic and Social Evolution of Latin America*, p. 203.

[5] 'The United States should recognize the significance and the role of CECLA as an effective vehicle of independent expression for the other American nations'. Nelson A. Rockefeller, *The Rockefeller Report on the Americas. The Official Report of a United States Presidential Mission for the Western Hemisphere*. New York Times Edition (Chicago: Quadrangle Books, 1969), p. 54.

[6] Few new investments are being undertaken in extractive activities. At the same time, disinvestment has been taking place in, for example, petroleum in Venezuela, and nationalizations have taken place in Cuba, Chile, and Peru, which are reflected in the statistics.

[7] *The Rockefeller Report*, pp. 45–6.

[8] In 1950, as part of the Marshall Plan, the United States appropriated $500 million to support a programme for liberalizing trade and payments in Europe. At Punta del Este the United States agreed to 'endow the Pre-Investment Fund for the Integration of Latin America', the only purpose of which was to carry out studies.

Chapter 8

The Renewed Importance of Europe

NEXT AFTER THE United States, western Europe is the region with which Latin America has the strongest links. Commercial activity between the two regions has now largely recovered from the decline that it underwent during and immediately after the war; by 1970 western Europe was purchasing about 35 per cent of all Latin American exports and supplying roughly a quarter of the foreign direct investment in the region, excluding petroleum and banking. Financial relations between the two regions, on the other hand, have yet to be more fully developed.

Of the Latin American countries, Argentina and Uruguay rely the most on West European capital and markets, while for Peru, Central America, and Colombia, Europe is less important. The West European countries that participate most in trade and investment in Latin America are Germany, Italy, Britain, the Netherlands, and France. All these countries are now members of the European Economic Community (EEC) (Britain since the beginning of 1973). The renewed economic importance of western Europe for Latin America can therefore be viewed best through an examination of the region's relations with the EEC, particularly since the Community is empowered to determine the trade policy of its members. Perhaps the largest unknown elements in these relations are the effects that Britain's entry will have on Latin American trade.

Of the European nations that are not members of the EEC, those with which Latin America has the most important economic relations are Sweden, Switzerland, and the Iberian countries. Trade with Sweden is well balanced, but in the case of Switzerland, the region's imports are much greater than its exports. Of total Swedish private investment and lending to less developed countries, over 65 per cent went to Latin America in 1968 and 1969. Some fifty Swedish manufacturing enterprises operate in Latin America, with an overall investment amounting to $110 million. Switzerland is similarly involved in Latin America, and the total

Latin American Trade with Western Europe* Selected Years
($ million)

	1961			1965			1970		
	Exports	Imports	Balance	Exports	Imports	Balance	Exports	Imports	Balance
Total Western Europe	2,674.0	2,711.4	−37.4	3490.4	2601.3	+889.1	4938.6	4302.1	+636.5
Enlarged EEC	2,300.1	2,253.6	+46.5	2896.6	2124.5	+772.1	3953.0	3371.8	+581.2
Original EEC	1,561.6	1,691.6	−130.0	2150.1	1644.0	−506.1	3179.8	2657.6	+522.2
Germany	542.7	839.4	−296.7	741.0	803.4	−62.4	1221.5	1336.2	−114.7
Italy	236.0	299.0	−63.0	447.0	298.8	+148.2	710.5	478.2	−232.3
France	174.1	245.5	−71.4	238.5	242.0	−3.5	395.8	416.8	−21.0
Benelux	608.8	307.7	+301.1	723.6	299.8	+423.8	852.0	426.4	+425.6
Britain	688.3	476.6	+211.7	672.9	422.7	+250.2	662.9	639.6	+23.3
Sweden	117.4	138.3	−20.9	178.6	142.8	+35.8	211.4	211.8	−0.4
Switzerland	32.3	143.2	−110.9	61.4	149.5	−88.1	102.8	287.9	−185.1
Spain	102.3	49.3	+53.0	194.9	71.2	+123.7	348.7	247.5	+101.2
Portugal	11.7	11.7	0.0	18.2	10.6	+7.6	25.9	21.9	+4.0

* Trade figures from Latin American sources.
Source: IMF, Direction of Trade.

of Swiss investment in the region exceeds $500 million, or 60 per cent of all Swiss investments in less developed countries.

Cultural propinquity, and continued emigration to Latin American countries, make the Iberian Peninsula – taking Spain and Portugal together – Latin America's fifth most important West European trade partner. Portugal's trade is small, and heavily concentrated on Brazil; but Spain has been prompted by her significant economic progress during the past decade, and by her exclusion from the EEC, to look more and more towards Latin America for markets.

Spain began to increase her exports of manufactured goods to Latin America and her purchases of Latin American primary products from the beginning of the 1960s. By 1965 Cuba was Spain's principal trading partner. Spain concluded an agreement for purchases of Cuban sugar, and since 1964 has signed several agreements with Argentina, mainly for buying meat. Trade with Spain is conducted to a large extent on the basis of bilateral payments agreements with individual Latin American countries; there is scope for broader economic relations. Spain's level of development and industrialization is similar to that of the larger Latin American countries, hence multilateral arrangements with the Latin American regional economic groups might prove fruitful. Among the possibilities that could be explored are some type of association with LAFTA and CACM, and participation in the payments agreements of both Spain and Portugal.

For western Europe as a whole, imports from Latin America represent a decreasing proportion of total imports. However, since 1961 Latin America has usually recorded trade surpluses with western Europe, even though European exports to Latin America have been rising at a faster pace than those of the United States. It would take only a slight accentuation of the present trade trends for Europe again to become a market of greater importance than the United States for Latin American products. This eventuality will, however, depend to a large extent on the trade policies followed by the enlarged EEC.

I. THE ENLARGED EEC

After the Second World War, when Europe was in the phase of reconstruction, trade with Latin America again began to gather momentum, mainly through bilateral arrangements, which were then the basis of Europe's foreign trade.

Assisted by the Marshall Plan, European leaders were able to carry out the reconstruction of the continent. They were determined to avoid the errors of the 1930s, when bilateralism, inconvertibility, barter trade, tariff and other restrictions, and so forth, had been widespread; they therefore concentrated on efficiency in production, and emphasized the need for outward-looking trade and financial policies through the liberalization of trade in manufactures, a multilateral payments system, and a progressively free movement of capital.[1] Subsequently in 1958 Belgium, France, West Germany, Italy, Luxembourg, and the Netherlands signed the Treaty of Rome. Britain for various reasons did not adhere to the treaty, but countered by forming the European Free Trade Association (EFTA) with Austria, Denmark, Norway, Portugal, Sweden, and Switzerland. The economic success of the EEC, and the disintegration of what was left of the British Commonwealth, persuaded policy-makers in Britain that there was no real alternative; despite many dissenting voices, Britain, together with Denmark and Ireland, has now entered the EEC.

Between 1958–60 and 1968–70, Latin American exports to the original member countries of the EEC grew at a higher annual rate than total Latin American exports. Nevertheless, Latin America's share of total EEC imports fell during the period from nearly 10 per cent to less than 7.5 per cent, a trend which is continuing. Not only has there been this overall decline, but, as statistics of Latin American exports by type of product show, there have been price fluctuations, mainly in temperate agricultural products and industrial raw materials. Some of these price changes are the consequence of the adoption of the EEC Common Agricultural Policy, which has radically affected long-standing economic relations between members of the Community and some of the Latin American countries.

European exports to Latin America, on the other hand, have increased in a more uniform and constant manner, so that the EEC has maintained a share of about 20 per cent of Latin America's imports. This has been accomplished partly through the European countries' export credit policies, which have counterbalanced Latin America's tendency to look to the United States for its imports. However, the relatively onerous conditions of these credits increased Latin America's indebtedness to Europe to the extent that many of the Latin American countries' debt-refinancing negotiations have to be carried out primarily with Europe.

In general, the lack of easier financial arrangements in Europe has resulted in current account balances with Latin American countries normally being in Europe's favour.[2] Latin America continues basically to export traditional primary products and is unable substantially to improve the trade balance with Europe. Very recently Brazil and Argentina have begun to export to countries such as West Germany and Italy, manufactures consisting chiefly of engineering components produced by the Latin American subsidiaries of trans-national corporations. Latin American exports to Germany and Italy have been increasing at a fairly rapid pace, though the region's share of the total imports of those countries has decreased substantially, as is also the case with almost every industrialized country. Latin American exports to Britain have remained more or less stagnant, because that country's trade has expanded at a slower rate than that of any other industrialized country. Britain's exports to Latin America have grown at about the same rate as overall British exports, but Britain's share of Latin America's imports has declined along with the general trend in Britain's external trade. Latin America's apparently very favourable trade balance with the Benelux countries is rather deceptive, since much of it represents goods that are re-exported.

European private direct investment has resumed a significant role in Latin America, and is being channelled mainly towards manufacturing industry rather than towards the public service industries where it held pre-eminence before the First World War. Unlike investment from the United States, European investment has hitherto come on the whole from the larger firms.

As with trade, the quantity and pattern of private foreign investment varies considerably from country to country. To take the two extremes, Britain, who was the leading European investor in Latin America before the Second World War, has had to relinquish this role in consequence of persistent payments deficits and problems related with the reserve currency role of sterling. Official exchange controls and taxation policies discourage capital outflows, with the inevitable result of a decrease in the rate of growth of British investment in Latin America.

In contrast with Britain during the past decade, West Germany has become the most important European exporter of capital to Latin America; the total of German direct private investment in the region has more than trebled in the course of these ten years, even though West Germany (like the United States) has directed this type of investment more towards the industrialized countries than to Latin America. Until recently it was only the largest German corporations that invested in Latin America, but medium-sized firms have now begun to show great interest in participating in joint ventures with Latin American entrepreneurs.[3]

At present, financial flows from Europe to Latin America are characterized by the predominance of credits to promote exports, but the conditions on which these are granted may be unsuitable in the light of Latin American balance-of-payments difficulties. Official bilateral assistance has represented less than 10 per cent of the total of commercial credit received by Latin America in the past decade; on the other hand, private capital markets, notably the Euro-dollar and Euro-bond markets, have not been sufficiently exploited by Latin America.

Greater use of these markets, either directly by individual countries or even enterprises, or through the Inter-American Development Bank, could entail a major expansion of Europe's relations with Latin America. However, financial transactions of this kind, as well as the real possibilities of wider European direct investment in the region, will only be able to materialize if trade between the two continents expands at a faster rate than up to now.

II. EUROPEAN TRADE POLICIES

The basic trade problems that concern Latin America are the EEC Common Agricultural Policy, the mounting number of preferential agreements negotiated with third countries (which increase the discrimination affecting Latin American products), and the extension of the preferential area that is occurring with the enlargement of the EEC.

The Common Agricultural Policy established by the original members of the Community is based on a procedure of fixing internal agricultural prices that ensure reasonable rewards for Community producers and therefore tend to be higher than those of the international market. The maintenance of these prices is assured through a mechanism of duly guaranteed intervention prices combined with the application of duties and variable levies (*prélèvements*) to imports to equate the market price of imported goods with the internal guaranteed prices.[4]

The complex machinery of protection for the agricultural sector of the EEC has seriously affected internal prices for agricultural products; rising food prices are a major cause of the high rates of inflation that the European countries have been experiencing since the beginning of the 1970s. The worst effect of the system, however, has been the increasing uncertainty that third-country suppliers have had to face. Some of them, including the Latin American countries, have been traditionally important suppliers of Europe for many decades. To a large measure these countries have now become merely marginal suppliers of the EEC, much to the detriment of their production and export structure.

The basic premise of the Baumgartner-Pisani Plan put forward by France in 1961 was that the agricultural policy of the EEC should be directed mainly to encouraging the organization of international markets; suppliers outside the Community would benefit as well as member countries. The way in which the plan has been put into effect has, however, produced just the opposite result. For certain important products, such as wheat and sugar, there are now greater imbalances than formerly, and in the case of milk and butter, subsidizing led to domestic surpluses that had to be dumped on world markets, to the detriment of many producing countries.

In 1969 the cost of agricultural subsidies paid out of public funds, and the inflated prices that consumers had to pay, meant that the Common Agricultural Policy represented a burden on the Community of some 3 per cent of its members' g.n.p., that is,

Price Comparisons for some Agricultural Products, 1968
(dollars per 100 kilogrammes)

Products	EEC*	United† Kingdom	EEC % excess 1 over 2	Quotations in the principal producing countries	EEC % excess 1 over 4
	1	2	3	4	5
Wheat	9.38	6.43	46	4.91[a]	91
Maize	8.78			4.46[a]	97
Beef and veal (live weight)	66.18	44.35	49	40.56[b]	63
Pig meat (live weight)	66.17	45.19	46	44.04[a]	50
Butter	181.72[c]	70.87[d]	156	70.87[d]	156
Sugar	21.33[e]	11.28[f]	89	4.87[g]	338

* Balanced average of prices received by the producers in the EEC countries including subsidies.
† Average of prices received by the producers, including subsidies.
[a] Chicago quotation.
[b] Copenhagen quotation.
[c] Balanced average of wholesale prices in the EEC.
[d] Import prices London/Retail prices New Zealand.
[e] Intervention prices.
[f] Commonwealth Sugar Agreement, contract prices.
[g] London quotation, average of three months.

Source: Pierre Uri (Rapporteur), *A Future for European Agriculture. A Report by a Panel of Experts* (Paris: Atlantic Institute, 1970).

between $11,000 million and $13,000 million, which is equivalent to half the value of their total agricultural production.[5]

The size of this burden on the European countries, which is in effect a vast misallocation of resources, makes it reasonable to suppose that the policy will be changed in the coming years. The European countries should give their agricultural producers adequate protection, but they should do so through a programme that also provides for the reorganization and modernization of agriculture, as does the policy traditionally followed in Britain and now perhaps to be modified. Such a scheme was envisaged in the Mansholt Plan, which was approved by the six founder members of the EEC after several years of discussion and against strong opposition from the agricultural sector.

Until the basic principles of the Common Agricultural Policy are changed, and a system based on direct support to the producer is set up, the situation can hardly be expected to improve.[6] When a change is introduced, part of the funds that would be released could well be allocated to investment in modernizing agriculture and restructuring industrial production so as to maintain adequate growth patterns that would stimulate international trade, make protective policies less necessary, and depend less on imported labour.

It is the temperate agricultural produce of Latin America that is chiefly affected by the EEC Common Agricultural Policy. Tropical products are affected by internal taxes in the Community which, by raising the consumer price, have had an adverse effect on the volume of consumption. In 1969, the Community countries were receiving about $500 million in taxes on coffee alone. Germany was still operating an internal tax on coffee of 125 per cent, and in Italy the internal tax was 152 per cent.

When the Treaty of Rome was drawn up in 1958, the Community favoured its members' former colonies (mainly in Africa) with preferential treatment. Though it could reasonably be claimed that in view of economic conditions in some of those countries this treatment was necessary, its extension to many other countries that have become eligible with Britain's entry is contrary to the letter and the spirit of the GATT. Moreover, it contravenes the agreement on the gradual elimination of such arrangements subscribed to by the original members of the EEC and other countries, in line with the recommendation in Annex A.II.1 of the final act of UNCTAD I.

Britain's entry into the EEC poses for Latin America both a potential threat and a hope. The extension of a community association agreement of the Yaoundé type to the developing countries of the Commonwealth could be detrimental to Latin America's exports, and could also be a major step towards an undesirable vertical division of international economic relations, which is a possibility that Latin America has always vigorously opposed on principle. Furthermore, the application of the Common Agricultural Policy to new EEC members will reduce the prospects of expanding Latin American agricultural exports to Britain, who has traditionally been the largest European importer of food products from the region. On the other hand, it is to be hoped that Britain's traditional reliance on world trade, and her well established system of subsidizing agriculture, will influence the trade policies of the enlarged Community in a more liberal direction.[7]

III. MOVING TOGETHER

Latin America should pay more attention to Europe than it has done in the past; it can learn something from Europe's experience, especially in regional economic integration. The members of the enlarged Community have also been, and are, important economic partners, and Latin America cannot ignore the problems posed by its economic relations with Europe, as it seems to have done by accepting in practically total silence the entry of Britain into the Community. This event has passed almost unnoticed, and there has been no serious attempt to evaluate the consequences that it will have on the Latin American countries: at both the national and the inter-American level this fact has aroused minimal interest.

Latin America's development problems today differ in many respects from the problems of European reconstruction in the first post-war decade. Even so, the economic policies that European recovery required, particularly the achievement of a common market, are very relevant to the region. As Latin America has now, Europe had then to contend with widely differing countries, powerful vested interests, and divergent levels of industrialization, such as those of Germany and Italy. It is interesting to recall that grave doubts existed in Italy after the war as to the wisdom of attempting to become integrated with more developed and industrialized countries, such as Germany, but in the event she has benefited enormously from economic association.[8]

Some major questions remain to be negotiated between Latin America and Europe if economic relations are to be closer in the future, and particularly if trade between the two regions is to expand. Besides the revision of some EEC trade policies, the basic requirements for the development of satisfactory and diversified

trade between Latin America and the enlarged Community include more appropriate overall financing terms, and increased
opportunities for Latin America's exports of manufactures and
semi-manufactures to Europe.

A first step towards securing better financial relations would be
the full participation of Europe in the Inter-American Development Bank and the Inter-American Committee on the Alliance for
Progress, of which more will be said in Chapter 10. The generalized
preferences for manufactures granted by the countries of the enlarged EEC to the developing countries, including Latin America,
are a gesture in the right direction, though, as will be pointed out
in Chapter 11, the impact of these preferences is much smaller
than is commonly supposed. There is, however, reason to believe
that some of the EEC countries would respond favourably to a
growth of imports of various classes of Latin American manufactured articles, if only because of the extreme difficulty of expanding exports to the region solely on the basis of increasing purchases
of its primary products. To take advantage of these opportunities,
Latin America must be capable of exporting to the European
market products that comply with required standards as regards
quality, quantity, and promptness of delivery.

A crucial question in future relations between Latin America
and the enlarged EEC is that of setting up adequate negotiating
machinery. Though individual Latin American countries sent
representatives to Brussels quite early on, for several years there
was no common Latin American approach to the EEC. This was
because there was no Latin American regional organization equivalent to the EEC, through which a joint representation could have
been made. The EEC, for its part, was slow to establish a common
policy towards Latin America. Many other issues inevitably took
precedence, and the attitudes of member countries towards Latin
America differed considerably one from another.

There were various efforts at institutionalizing contacts between
the Community and Latin America, but none of them was successful. It was not until November 1968 that a memorandum to the
Ministerial Council of the EEC from the Italian government
inspired greater interest in Latin America. As a result, in July
1969, the Commission published a report on relations with the
Latin American countries, emphasizing the need for the European
countries to inform one another of their policies towards Latin
America, to link the trade and financial aspects of their policies,
and to lend support to integration within the region.

The Latin American countries responded through CECLA in
the Declaration of Buenos Aires of July 1970. This appealed for

greater access to the EEC for Latin American exports, a larger flow of capital as well as facilities for financing Latin American exports, and scientific and technological co-operation. In May 1971 a 'mécanisme de dialogue' was set up which provided for periodic meetings between representatives of Latin America and of the Common Market. This is not enough, however, and it now remains for Latin America to negotiate, through a reorganized CECLA, the setting-up of more effective contacts.

NOTES

[1] The principal organizations through which economic recovery was achieved included the OEEC, the UN Economic Commission for Europe (ECE), and the European Payments Union (EPU), which played a vital role during the post-war years in preparing the machinery for closer economic integration.

[2] The situation emerges differently if the trade balance is calculated on the basis of Latin American figures or if EEC figures are used, not only because Latin American exports f.o.b. appear as c.i.f. imports in the EEC figures, but also because of time lapses, and deficiencies in statistics.

[3] For a detailed analysis see reports of the annual meetings of the Institut für Ibero-Amerika Kunde for 1970–71 and 1972, and Jürgen Westphalen, *América Latina y Europa* (Hamburg: Übersee Verlag, 1971).

[4] This mechanism is in fact more complex than this outline implies: for the majority of products there is an indicative price which itself has two parts (one for production and one for the market) and another intervention price, which in some cases is a minimum guaranteed price for the producer. The Council of Ministers fixes these prices annually at levels that have risen steadily in recent years. There are also minimum prices for imports, which are modified several times during each year.

[5] $7,000 million of public funds were paid out in subsidies, of which $2,000 million came from the tax levies on imports, thus indirectly from consumers.

[6] For a complete analysis of the system applied by the EEC, the great distortions it has created, and proposals as to how the system could be changed in order to obtain real protection for European farmers without affecting world trade, especially the developing countries, see Pierre Uri, Rapporteur, *A Future for European Agriculture. A Report by a Panel of Experts* (Paris: Atlantic Institute, 1970).

[7] The traditional British method of protecting agrarian incomes has been through deficiency payments, which are direct subsidies given to producers, to make up the difference between the market prices of cheap imports and the official support prices. In the interest of consumers, imports have been allowed in with few restrictions, other than sanitary requirements, and at low rates of duty. The cost of the subsidy is borne by the taxpayers, according to their income, while food prices remain low.

[8] In 1951, 42 per cent of Italian manpower was still employed in agriculture. By 1968, this figure had been reduced to 21 per cent. As Guido Carli has pointed out, 'more than a few thought that Italy should not align herself with highly industrialized economies...The facts have refuted them categorically; our foreign trade has notably benefited from incorporation with a highly industrialized zone... Instead of falling into a situation of permanent difficulty with the balance of payments, the evolution of our accounts with foreign countries has been highly favourable'. Instituto Italo-Latino Americano, ed., *América Latina, Italia y la Comunidad Económica Europea* (Milan: Giuffrè, 1968), p. 144.

Chapter 9

Broadening Relations with Other Industrialized Countries

LATIN AMERICA HAS not only maintained its important economic links with the United States and revived its traditional ties with western Europe, but has also been establishing relations with the other industrialized countries. This development is of the utmost importance to the region's prospects of participating more fully in the world economy in the coming years.

The most important of these new partners is Japan, whose contacts with Latin America date back at least to the early decades of this century, when many Japanese immigrants came to Latin America; today there are some 700,000 Japanese-Latin Americans. It is only since the Second World War, however, that economic relations between Latin America and Japan have taken firm root. The recent rapid development of Japan's economy and her acute lack of natural resources mean that both in trade and in investment Latin America and Japan have much to offer each other. At the same time, since transport has become more efficient, the distances involved are today less significant than formerly.

Latin America also has much to gain from stronger links with other industrialized countries, and has already made a beginning with Canada and with the European socialist countries. Up to now Latin American trade relations with the socialist world have been concentrated on the Comecon group. Recently there has been a slight increase in trade with China, but though further expansion would be very desirable for Latin America, it seems unlikely that there will be any significant increase for some time. The prospects for expanding trade with Yugoslavia, a European socialist country outside the Comecon group, are good, however, and Latin America would do well to adopt a more active approach to trade with that country.

The outlook for broader economic ties is brighter still in the case of Australia and New Zealand. It is not always remembered that

Latin America has a Pacific seaboard that stretches from Tijuana in northern Mexico to Cape Horn at the southern tip of the continent, and is longer than that of the United States. Australia and New Zealand are natural partners for the Latin American countries, particularly those with a Pacific coast, who should intensify their present rather slender contacts with these two countries.

Latin American Trade with Various Countries and Regions
($ million)

	Exports from Latin America			Imports into Latin America		
	1961	1965	1970	1961	1965	1970
Australia	10.5	9.1	17.4	10.8	29.4	39.4
Canada	147.8	347.4	463.2	194.1	262.9	454.3
China	7.0	96.2	2.7	0.8	1.4	1.3
Japan	275.6	427.6	962.1	281.1	383.7	870.6
New Zealand	11.4	4.6	0.1	3.7	4.8	10.1
Socialist Countries	144.6	304.4	318.3	138.6	134.0	131.2
Yugoslavia	14.2	32.2	60.5	6.3	10.3	20.6

Source: IMF, Direction of Trade.

The reinforcing of Latin America's economic relations with the industrialized countries by no means implies that the region should neglect to establish firm links with the developing countries of the Middle East, Africa, and Asia. Indeed, the stronger its economic relations with the industrialized countries, the better Latin America will be able to develop relations with these other regions, on either a bilateral or a multilateral basis. Latin America should not be deterred by the rather rudimentary state of communications within the 'Third World', which will certainly present some difficulties to begin with. As time goes on there will be increasing opportunities for Latin America to join with the other developing regions in fruitful economic co-operation.

1. JAPAN: A CONVERGENCE OF INTERESTS

In the past decade, there has been a rapid expansion in economic relations between Latin America and Japan. The value of trade more than quadrupled, and private medium-term and long-term financing for imports from Japan now exceeds $200 million a year. The trade balance is slightly favourable to Latin America, since the region's exports to Japan have increased at a rather higher rate than its imports from Japan. Though the growth in Latin American exports to Japan may seem impressive, they represent a decreasing proportion of Japan's total imports, which have grown at an unusually fast and sustained rate, reflecting the country's remarkable economic growth. Latin America's share of total Japanese imports declined from 8.8 per cent in 1956–58 to 6.2 per cent in 1968–70. Even so, the growth in absolute values was appreciable.

Latin American Trade with Japan

	Latin American Exports to Japan f.o b.	Latin American Imports from Japan c.i. f.
1960	195.0	211.2
1962	280.9	313.0
1964	422.3	312.7
1966	491.8	411.0
1968	616.5	510.4
1969	736.5	660.2
1970	962.1	870.6

Source: IMF, *Direction of Trade.*

The failure of Japan's imports from Latin America to keep pace with the expansion of total Japanese imports is attributable to several factors. Certainly Latin America could have acted more aggressively. The exports of many other regions (North America, Asia, Africa, the Middle East, the socialist countries, Australia and New Zealand) have risen faster than those of Latin America. Moreover, the greater part of these increases has been in primary products, which account for over 80 per cent of Japan's imports. Latin America's exports are also primary goods, but the region is at something of a disadvantage in that these exports are concentrated in food products (especially tropical foods and animal feeds) and mineral raw materials.

For minerals essential to her economy, Japan has long-established suppliers. In the case of iron ore, for instance, Australia gained a firm hold on the Japanese market before the 1950s. Only quite recently has Brazil started to penetrate the market, through mining enterprises undertaken jointly by the Brazilian government and Japanese firms. The ores of Chile and Peru are now at a further disadvantage because they contain a higher degree of sulphur than is permitted by Japan's new anti-pollution regulations.

The food products that Latin America is easily able to provide have been under restrictions in the Japanese market. Though the number of products subject to quantitative restrictions was reduced from 120 to 33 between 1969 and 1972, those still affected include important Latin American exports, such as beef, some kinds of fish, fruits, beverages, and dairy products.[1] Also, despite reductions in duties after the Kennedy Round and favourable treatment under the scheme of generalized preferences, the tariffs on many products of interest to Latin America remain quite high, particularly on processed foodstuffs. Processed beef products, for example received practically no favourable treatment in the generalized system of preferences that Japan accorded to Latin America in 1971. Some primary products are also still subject to a high tariff rate, among them bananas, sugar, pineapples, fresh beef, and roasted coffee.

Exports of manufactures from Latin America to Japan have been very small. Of a 1970 total of $130 million of exports classified as manufactures, over $100 million represent copper and its alloys, and most of the rest is made up of iron concentrates and semi-finished steel. This is very different from the situation of Asian countries that have established closer links with Japan, and to which Japan has begun to export industries. Exports of light manufactures, including textiles, from countries such as Korea and Taiwan to Japan have increased very rapidly in recent years. It is only very lately that Latin America, especially Brazil, has begun to make this type of arrangement with Japan.

Just as Japan's imports from Latin America have increased in absolute terms but decreased as a percentage of total Japanese imports, so Japan's exports to Latin America have risen absolutely but account for a smaller proportion of total Japanese exports. This trade also represents a much larger proportion of Latin American imports than it did a decade ago. In 1970, Japanese exports to Latin America represented over 7 per cent of the total imports of the region, compared with less than 4 per cent in 1960. At the same time a sharp change took place in the composition of these imports; for example, imports of light manufactures, including textiles, from Japan have been cut back to a larger extent in Latin America than in the United States, Canada, or Australia, because these are the industries that are most highly protected by the region's import substitution policies.

The extraordinary development of heavy industry in Japan has enabled the decline in exports of light manufactures to Latin America to be more than compensated. In the second half of the 1960s, exports of heavy industrial and chemical products were trebled, and now comprise 80 per cent of Japan's total exports to Latin America, while the share of light industrial products in the export total decreased from 30 per cent at the beginning of the last decade to 17 per cent in 1970. Even so, Japan's exports of capital goods to Latin America grew more slowly than those to the developing countries of Asia because, quite naturally, during the last decade Japan has established much stronger financial links with them, especially with regard to 'aid'. Also, capital goods cannot be introduced into new markets overnight, and Latin America was already accustomed to North American and European products. This obstacle has now been overcome, and Japan has major export markets in Brazil, Venezuela, Argentina, Mexico, Chile, Cuba, and Panama (which serves in part as an entrepôt) as well as markets of some importance in practically all the other continental and Caribbean countries.

Japanese direct investment in Latin America has increased faster than trade, chiefly because it has been taking advantage of opportunities offered by import substitution policies. The book value of Japanese investments increased from about $60 million in 1960 to $500 million in 1970, and now exceeds the value of French investment in the region. By 1969 direct investments by Japanese enterprises accounted for nearly 21 per cent of total foreign investment in Latin America.[2] Only in North America does Japan have a larger share (31 per cent) of her total foreign investment. Furthermore, Japanese sources estimate that the value of Japanese direct investment in Latin America will exceed those of Britain and West Germany by the mid-1970s.[3] The largest portion (about half) of this investment is in the manufacturing sector, where it is involved in a wide range of activities. The proportion is high compared with Japanese direct investment in the same sector in Asia, which amounts to only about one-third of the total. Mining accounts for another 11 per cent and construction another 5 per cent of Japanese direct investment in Latin America, which is heavily concentrated in Brazil (51 per cent), Chile and Peru (10 per cent each), Mexico (6.5 per cent), and Argentina (5 per cent).

The prospects for further expansion of Latin America's economic relations with Japan seem excellent. The present pattern of trade cannot, however, provide the basis for satisfactory and enduring economic links between Latin America and Japan. Their relations should not continue to be based almost exclusively on the combination of Latin American exports of primary products and Japanese investment in import substitution, which too closely resembles the overworked formula for Latin America's present relations with the United States and Europe.

There are many factors on both sides that favour much closer, and mutually beneficial, economic co-operation. Japan can benefit from Latin America's abundant raw materials and foodstuffs, of which the Japanese will have increasing need. At the same time, the level of industrialization attained by Latin America furnishes it with skills and facilities that make it a very attractive region for the establishment of industries to export to Japan and elsewhere.

Latin America, for its part, should take note of the enormous expansion that is taking place in the Japanese import market, particularly since this market is also changing in a direction that is highly advantageous to Latin America. The demand for imported foodstuffs is rising at a faster rate than the g.n.p.; Japan is having to rely more on imported industrial raw materials; the problems of pollution are worsening; scarcity of labour, though not yet acute, is becoming noticeable.

The rapid increase in the demand for food imports will be maintained for some time, because it stems from long-term factors peculiar to Japan. First, the total amount of food consumed is still low compared with that of Western countries, so there remains much room for expansion. Second, the traditional diet, consisting mainly of fish, rice, local fruits, and beverages, is being replaced by a greater consumption of bread, meat, tropical fruits, and beverages, which Japan either does not produce at all or produces in only small quantities. Both factors are likely to be accentuated as the Japanese come increasingly under Western influence, acquire more purchasing power, and wish to vary their diet.

The demand for imports of raw materials has also risen much faster in Japan than in other industrialized countries. This is due to the extreme scarcity of natural resources in Japan, and to the major contribution that the manufacturing sector is making to the rapid increase in the g.n.p. In all likelihood a mounting proportion of the raw materials that Japan buys abroad will have to be imported as finished or semi-finished goods, rather than in their primary form. This practice will be forced on Japan by the increasing scarcity of labour and by the need to reduce industrial pollution of the environment.

The shortage of manpower that Japan is beginning to feel is reflected in the rapid rise in wages of recent years. According to the Japanese Ministry of Labour, between 1965 and 1970 real wages rose by 54.6 per cent. The additional labour force created by the population bulge of the immediate post-war period has already been absorbed and the demand for manpower is still increasing, as the economic boom continues; Japan's labour shortage is therefore likely to become more acute. This is making several Japanese industries less competitive, not only in foreign markets, but also in the domestic market, and it seems inevitable that a radical adjustment will occur in Japan's industrial production. Clearly, there are many good reasons for Japanese financial and commercial interests to join with Latin American governments and private sectors in setting up a new and dynamic pattern of economic relations. In particular, the raw materials and foodstuffs that Japan needs could be exported from Latin America in processed form, with the maximum possible value added in Latin America. Japan and Latin America should also co-operate in organizing their industrial production in such a way as to complement each other, Japan importing certain manufactures in exchange for her exports of capital equipment and heavy chemicals.

The establishment of this new pattern would require several specific initiatives. The Latin American countries should be more active in seeking long-term contracts with Japan, similar to those that Japan has made with Australia. Brazil has already made progress in this direction by arranging, for example, the mining, processing, and exporting to Japan of iron ore, with the active participation of Brazil's state enterprises. Latin American initiatives of this kind would be welcomed by Japanese industrialists who need reliable supplies of industrial raw materials and fuels and prefer to obtain them through participating directly with producers, rather than to buy them from the trans-national corporations of other industrialized countries that specialize in marketing them.

Latin America should achieve a greater involvement in some of Japan's industrial processes, either through direct investment in joint ventures or through technical assistance. Japanese enterprises could assign to Latin American firms the manufacture of components for articles that would be difficult to produce as finished goods in Latin America. Of special interest would be industries in which Japan has the advantage of a high level of technology, such as electronics, precision instruments, machinery, motor vehicles and ship-building. A major benefit of such arrangements would be that Latin American firms would become familiar with Japanese technology, which has been developed to use more labour and less capital than do the technologies of the United States and some European countries. Furthermore, Japan has gained experience in this form of co-operation from similar undertakings with neighbouring countries.

It would also be desirable that Japan should lower tariffs on several classes of industrial goods; some tariffs are high in Japan compared with other industrialized nations, and in effect represent a relatively high degree of protection. These are mainly goods that are currently being made in Japan with raw materials imported from Latin America, such as textiles, leather goods, metals, and alloys, as well as processed foods, all of which could easily be produced in Latin America. Some other industrial products requiring a higher degree of technology should also be given better access to the Japanese market, so that Latin America could export them; this would call for supplementary measures, one of which would be Japanese financial and technical co-operation.

Japan's bilateral assistance, as defined by the Development Assistance Committee of the OECD and including contributions to the Inter-American Development Bank, has hitherto been small. It would be realistic to gear future Japanese financial assistance to promoting new trade patterns, as Japan is already doing with some Asian countries through projects called *kaihatsu yunyu* (development and imports). Japan should undertake such projects on a multilateral basis as well as with individual countries. To this end it is desirable that Japan become a subscribing member of the Inter-American Development Bank, through which she could channel more financial resources to Latin America. More will be said of this in Chapter 10.

The concentration of Japanese export efforts in the United States market has caused an adverse reaction there and prompted a protectionist trend. Japan's commercial aggressiveness is likely to evoke a similar response in other industrialized countries if she does not diversify her economic links. In her relations with the developing countries of South-East Asia, Japan faces similar problems; her share in the market of most of them is already quite large, and these countries are beginning to be wary of becoming yet more dependent on Japan. This state of affairs is favourable to an expansion of economic ties between Latin America and Japan. Furthermore, Japan's dependence on imports has made her adopt an official attitude to foreign trade that is both liberal and global and coincides with the interests of Latin America.[4]

II. CANADA: AN ADDED DIMENSION TO
INTER-AMERICAN RELATIONS

Canada, like Latin America, faces certain problems that spring from being a neighbour of the United States and from having a very strong economic nexus with that country. Canada shares Latin America's desire to counterbalance the influence of the

United States, and is actively seeking to expand her economic relations with other countries. Latin America has always been ready to welcome greater involvement with Canada, particularly in the inter-American institutions, where the region feels most need to offset the predominance of the United States. While the United States and Latin America were in such close harness, Canada was chary of participating in the inter-American system for fear of having to align herself with either the United States or Latin America, thus antagonizing one or the other.

Towards the end of the 1960s, Canada's long-standing interest in Latin America became more active, and in November 1968 an important Canadian ministerial mission was sent to Latin America. Its report stressed that :

In addition to Canada's traditional exports Canada is clearly in a position to participate much more fully in the economic and industrial development of Latin American countries.

Soon afterwards the Canadian government undertook a major review of its foreign policy. The conclusions were published in September 1970 in a document comprising six sections, one of which was devoted to Latin America. In the light of the changes occurring in relations between the United States and Latin America, several proposals were made for involving Canada in the deliberations and institutions of the inter-American system. As a result, in 1971 Canada became a full member of the Inter-American Development Bank, with a share of 4 per cent of the capital, and at the beginning of 1972 was admitted as a permanent observer to the Organization of American States.

The foreign policy document also recommended that greater efforts be made to expand economic relations, particularly trade, with Latin America. One of the most interesting suggestions, which could be very helpful to Latin American exporters of non-traditional manufactured products, was that Canada should second to the region specialists experienced in the various techniques of exporting. The Latin American countries should grasp every opportunity of increasing exports to Canada, since most of them have an adverse trade balance with that country. Except for petroleum and petroleum products from Venezuela, which become re-exports to the United States, Canadian imports from Latin America (including Cuba) have grown very slowly during the post-war period. Canadian exports to Latin America have, however, increased from about $100 million a year in the early 1950s to about $450 million in 1970.[5]

Latin America and Selected Latin American Countries: Trade with Canada

($ million)

Country	1961		1965		1970	
	Exports	Imports	Exports	Imports	Exports	Imports
LATIN AMERICA	147.8	194.1	347.4	262.9	463.2	454.3
Argentina	2.5	30.4	5.9	30.4	6.6	49.3
Brazil	18.8	26.2	46.2	12.9	47.3	98.2
Mexico	5.8	33.5	9.2	37.7	12.0	49.4
Venezuela	93.3	41.0	246.4	83.7	325.0	107.6

Source: IMF, Direction of Trade.

To some extent, the poor growth of Latin America's exports to Canada is explained by the fact that Canada herself produces many of the minerals and temperate agricultural products that Latin America has to offer. Furthermore, Canada imports tropical products from long-established suppliers within the Commonwealth. All the same, the Canadian market is relatively free, with few import restrictions and either low or non-existent tariffs for many products that Latin America can export. It should be possible for the countries of Latin America to export much more to Canada if they were to make a determined attack on the market. Canada has every reason to join with the region in promoting both traditional exports, and particularly in devising formulas to facilitate Latin American exports of manufactures, since an expansion of trade in both directions must benefit both trading partners.

Though there have been a few major Canadian investments in Latin America, and these have been limited to a small group of large corporations, they have made substantial exports – either regularly or from time to time as circumstances allowed – of wheat, newsprint, and, more recently, motor vehicle parts, aircraft, and various forms of fabricated metals and machinery. In the field of investment and the transfer of technology, Canada could cooperate more fully with Latin American enterprises in pioneering new forms of association with local capital and management contracts. Canada could make a most valuable contribution to setting up such arrangements, in view of her own experience with massive foreign investment and the problems and benefits that accompany it.

There is one other respect in which Latin America has much to gain from closer collaboration with Canada. Despite being a developed and largely industrialized country, Canada is still emerging; she has faced, and in some cases continues to face, many of the same development problems as does Latin America, in agriculture, mining, fisheries, forestry, long-distance transport, energy production, telecommunications, tourism, and other spheres. Canada has tackled these problems on a scale and in circumstances that often parallel those of Latin America. Moreover, her experience is sufficiently recent to make it especially relevant to Latin America. As Canada's export trade concentrates more and more on specialized and advanced technology and expertise, Latin America could derive great benefit from a flourishing interchange.

III. COMECON : OBSTACLES AND OPPORTUNITIES[6]

Latin America's interest in expanding economic relations with the East European socialist countries that form the Comecon has arisen from the need to broaden and diversify its international markets, for traditional and for new exports. So far these relations have evolved rather slowly, but there are good prospects of overcoming the various difficulties that have prevented trade from increasing at a faster pace. An encouraging sign has been given in the latest five-year (1971–75) plans of the socialist bloc, which give foreign trade greater importance among the factors of development.

Trade is still at a very low level mainly because, for most Latin American countries, Comecon countries do not export enough to be able to pay for the products that they wish to import from the region. The Latin American countries have for many years been accumulating trade surpluses that are large in relation to the total trade involved, and have resulted in favourable balances in the clearing accounts negotiated with individual Comecon countries. The East European countries repay these debts in goods, in hard currency, or through the transfer of credit to other socialist countries, but there are often long delays, which are detrimental to the sound development of trade.

Latin America* : Balance of Trade with Comecon Countries 1964–1970

($ million)

	1964	*1965*	*1966*	*1967*	*1968*	*1969*	*1970*
Exports (f.o.b.)	219.3	335.9	326.5	259.9	253.5	274.7	318
Imports (c.i.f.)	109.8	125.8	130.8	135.3	145	145	107
Balance	+109.5	+210.1	+195.7	+124.6	+110.5	+129.7	+201

* Excluding Cuba.
Source : National Statistics.

Latin American sources attribute the problems of trade with the Comecon countries to the difficulty of maintaining and repairing machinery and equipment produced in socialist countries because of differing technical standards, to protracted procedures for settling credit balances, and to other administrative delays. For their part, the East European countries consider that the problems stem from the small size of the Latin American market, which has not yet made it worth their while to set up efficient maintenance facilities for their machinery, and from Latin America's lack of confidence in their technology, which is due largely to ignorance of their levels of industrial competence.

Most of this trade is conducted within the framework of bilateral commercial agreements, which the nations of eastern Europe have been actively arranging with Latin America on the basis of their experience in recent decades with African and Asian governments. These agreements form part of the socialist countries' programmes of 'aid' to developing countries; the philosophy and the instruments bear some similarity to the inter-American programmes. Both aim at overcoming backwardness, raising standards of living, and pointing the way to self-sustaining development. To these ends, they provide means for the financing of social works and infrastructure, credit for the export of capital goods, technical assistance, and co-operation in development planning.

The essential substance of the agreements is that the socialist countries give credit to the Latin American countries while assuring for themselves imports of primary commodities needed by their

Credits Granted by Comecon Countries to Latin America 1967–71
($ million)

Destination Latin American country		Origin by Comecon country	
Argentina	30	Bulgaria	40
Bolivia	30	Czechoslovakia	85
Brazil	35	Hungary	75
Colombia	5	Poland	45
Chile	162	Romania	20
Ecuador	5	USSR	160
Peru	123		
Uruguay	35		
TOTAL	425		425

Source: Based on the commercial agreements and instruments signed by Latin American and Comecon countries.

economies. The Latin American countries have not always negotiated these agreements to their own best advantage, largely because they have been presented with situations with which they
were unfamiliar in dealing with credits for industrial equipment.
Also, as is occasionally alleged in socialist circles, Latin American
governments have sometimes, for reasons of internal political pres-
tige, attempted to negotiate credits for much larger sums than they
can use. During the period 1967–71, Latin America signed 41 basic
agreements with the countries of the Comecon and contracted
credits for buying equipment and other goods for a total value of
almost 425 million dollars.

These apparently substantial contractual and financial incentives
have not yet produced any great flow of trade. Administrative
shortcomings on both sides have caused delays and interruptions
in the procedures provided for the drawing-down of credits. Latin
America is hampered in using the credits by the fact that each is
tied to a specific socialist country. Moreover, in certain cases, they
turn out to be more costly than export credits from western Europe,
Japan, or the United States.

Both the accumulation by the Latin Americans of trade surpluses and the scant use made of credits reflect the up-hill struggle
of the socialist countries to export to Latin America. To ease
matters, some Comecon countries have decided to begin liquidating
transactions in convertible currency; the USSR has recently agreed
to end the clearing agreement with Brazil, and Czechoslovakia is
no longer maintaining clearing accounts with any Latin American
country.

Other, longer-term, arrangements could be set up. Active consideration should be given to making a multilateral clearing agreement between Latin America and the Comecon, which could be
managed by the Bank for Economic Co-operation and the Inter-
American Development Bank. The agreement could well encompass clearing balances not only between Latin American and
Comecon countries, but also through third countries, such as the
United States and Japan, which might expect to incur deficits with
the socialist countries in the future; this could occur if the
investment and trade agreements now being negotiated with the
United States and Japan come to fruition. Furthermore, if the
serious limitations on the use by Latin America of Comecon credits
were removed, they would be more fully used than they are now.
Credits should be untied by means of a financing pool maintained
by the Comecon countries as a bloc.

Latin America should also press for changes in the composition
of trade with the socialist countries, in which East European

manufactured goods and Latin American primary products, including some foodstuffs, continue to predominate. The opening-up of eastern Europe to Latin American manufactured products would enable Latin America to alter its trade more positively by basing it on the exchange of goods with a higher degree of value added.

The co-ordination of commercial policies among members of the Comecon means that these countries virtually form a unit in negotiations with Latin America. In contrast, in its relations with the socialist area, Latin America shows the lack of cohesion that has been a decisive weakness throughout its commercial policy. If Latin America is to achieve a fruitful expansion of economic relations with the socialist countries, it needs to establish, through the Special Committee for Latin American Co-ordination (CECLA), a common commercial policy and a permanent mechanism for negotiating with eastern Europe.

NOTES

[1] These 33 products may be imported to a value of 3 per cent of total internal consumption, and this will perhaps be increased to 5 per cent.

[2] Figures for investment taken from Saburo Okita, *Japan and Latin America: A Changing Economic Relation* (paper prepared for the Conference of the Pacific, Viña del Mar, 1970).

[3] Okita, *Japan and Latin America*.

[4] In *Economic Survey of Japan 1970–71* (Tokyo, July 1971), the Economic Stabilization Board identified four basic elements in the reorientation of Japan's trade policy: a major effort to safeguard free trade; an end to giving maximum priority to exports; fuller co-operation with developing countries; and control of increases in the trade surplus. On the third point it was stated 'Especially important [are] the qualitative improvement of assistance through expansion of technical assistance and easing of aid terms [and] promotion of economic development through trade expansion. It is necessary to open the Japanese market to products of developing nations through application of tariff preferences and other measures' (p. 97).

[5] In reading the figures, one should not forget that some Canadian companies ship goods to Latin America through United States marketing organizations, so that the latter's name appears in the statistical returns rather than that of the Canadian manufacturer. This incorporation of United States–Canadian ventures in Latin America extends to various sectors and often means that Canadian economic involvement in Latin America is underestimated.

[6] For lack of information, Cuba is not included in this analysis. It would be of the greatest interest for organizations such as ECLA thoroughly to study the experience of the one Latin American country that has broad economic relations with the socialist countries.

PART FOUR

Towards Interdependence

Chapter 10

Financing Development

RAPID CHANGES ARE occurring in international finance and overseas investment. The recovery of international capital markets outside the United States, and the possibility of linking aid to the creation of international liquidity, should modify the pattern of international development finance in the next few years.

Three recent developments in international investment will certainly be of great significance for some time to come : the growing participation in international markets of large and small firms from various industrialized countries; the rising interest of international firms in entering into service contracts; and the emergence of large trans-national corporations.[1] It is difficult at present to envisage all the consequences of these three developments. The emergence of powerful trans-national corporations creates political problems, but such enterprises could play a part in helping the developing countries and Latin America to expand their exports of manufactures, similar to their role in the industrialized countries. There are many ways in which developing countries can use these corporations to their advantage.

In the past 25 years significant changes have occurred in the world's financial and capital markets. At the end of the war and throughout the 1950s, the United States was virtually the sole source of financing and had the only international capital market. During the 1960s, however, the national capital markets in Europe and Japan regained their pre-war importance. Even though the European countries (including Britain) and Japan maintain many restrictions on financial and capital movements in their own currencies, they are now important centres of the world-wide Euro-dollar market, which constitutes an immense new source of funds for the financing of international investment.

At the same time that these new international financial possibilities have been opening up, the large industrial countries have been coming to accept, first, that a larger proportion of development assistance should be channelled through multilateral organizations, and second, that the creation of SDRs (special drawing rights) or any other form of international money should be linked to the financing of development.[2]

Were these two ideas implemented, the industrialized countries might come nearer to fulfilling their commitment to allocate to 'aid' one per cent of their g.n.p., as was requested of them at UNCTAD II. The reluctance of the industrialized countries to become closely involved in economic co-operation with developing countries has been manifest in their method of calculating their financial transfers when determining which of them comes closest to, or even exceeds, the 'moral goal' of one per cent of g.n.p. to which they have committed themselves. In these arithmetical measurements of international righteousness, which the developing countries seem rather surprisingly to have accepted as a genuine exercise in international co-operation, any business transaction or even any deal motivated by purely political interest qualifies as a helpful transfer for development. The term 'aid' may cover anything from foreign investment in general, to suppliers' credits, or transfers to overseas departments.[3]

This situation could be corrected if the trends towards multilateral financing, and the more automatic mechanism of SDRs, were combined with a more realistic goal for development assistance, which would be 0.70 per cent of g.n.p. for official development assistance. This was set forth by the Pearson Commission to dissipate the confusion created by the one per cent target, and has been taken up as an official goal by the United Nations.[4]

The easiest, and probably the most effective, way to use SDRs for development assistance would be, each time that they are created, to assign a portion to replenishing the loanable resources of the international and regional institutions. This notion has been opposed on the grounds that it is inflationary, but to the extent that it becomes a more automatic way of transferring resources that have in any case been committed, and are already being transferred in one way or another, by the industrialized countries, it would be no more inflationary than the creation of SDRs *per se*. It has also been objected that it would be difficult to establish a rational and politically acceptable set of rules for distributing SDRs among the international and regional financing agencies, but this difficulty could also be surmounted by allocating new SDRs among the regional banks in proportion to the IMF quotas (as modified in the course of the reform) of the developing countries of each area.

I. SETTING A FRESH COURSE

For the next decade, Latin America's gross external financing needs will continue to be sizeable, even if the region's exports make great strides in world markets. The relatively less developed countries – that is, the Central American and some Caribbean nations, Paraguay, and Bolivia – will continue to require real resource transfers to supplement their insufficient savings; all the Latin American countries will need external financial resources until they raise their export earnings to satisfactory levels; and all will require financial transfers to service their debt, which is dangerously large, especially for some of them.[5]

The industrialized countries have a stake in ensuring the external financing of the region during the 1970s. Latin America can become a very important economic partner of the industrialized countries in the future, but will require during the coming years adequate types of external assistance in establishing a sound foundation for the business pattern on which future economic relations will be based.

The external financing of economic development in Latin America therefore involves new problems and new prospects requiring new strategies. The basic aims of these strategies should be, first, to solve the debt problem, and second, to strengthen and broaden – on the lenders' side – the multinational base of the Inter-American Development Bank and the Caribbean Development Bank. The banks should be provided with more resources, both conventional and concessional; their structure should be made to reflect more accurately Latin America's trading relations; and they

Latin America, excluding Cuba and Venezuela
Current Account of the Balance of Payments, 1950–69
($ million)

	Balance of goods and services transactions	Balance of profits and interest payments (public and private)	Balance on current account
	ANNUAL AVERAGE		
1950–59	– 178	– 483	– 661
1960–64	– 530	– 825	– 1,330
1965–69	– 27	– 1,415	– 1,440

Source: ECLA, *Trends and Structures of the Latin American Economy* (Santiago, March 1971), p. 71.

should more fully draw on the various financial centres of the world.

Immediately after the war, in the five-year period 1946–50, Latin America's balance of goods and services transactions was on average favourable. Excluding Cuba and Venezuela, it amounted to more than $500 million annually. During the 1960s, however, the current account became increasingly adverse and countries required ever larger amounts of external financing.

The Alliance for Progress programme, which was conceived to respond to basic Latin American development problems, helped to bring about the transformation of Latin America's external insufficiency, which had originated in the slow growth of exports, into a 'spiral of external financial indebtedness'. During the 1960s, the region received external financing (both through the Alliance for Progress and from other sources) that permitted it to cover the deficits in its current accounts, but at the cost of growing public indebtedness, which rose from $2,213 million in 1950 to $6,631 million in 1960, and to somewhat over $20,000 million by the end of 1970 (including undrawn sums).[6]

A summary analysis of the international transactions of the six countries that accounted for 80 per cent of the public debt in Latin America in 1969 is illuminating.[7] The servicing of the public debt, including that contracted with official guarantees, in these countries is the factor that has most affected their international financial position, and has most contributed to restricting the room for manoeuvre in the management of their international economic policy.[8] As the following table shows, the servicing of the public debt in the late 1960s was almost equivalent to gross capital inflows, and so became the principal concern of their financial authorities.

Though the rate of growth of the public external debt in the

Servicing of Public Debt and
Gross Capital Inflow Requirements for Six Countries*
($ million)

	1 Servicing of public debt	2 Gross capital inflow requirements
1965	1,553	– 1,794
1967	1,879	– 2,289
1969	1,953	– 2,408

* Argentina, Brazil, Chile, Colombia, Mexico, and Peru.
Column 1 is the sum of interest and amortization payments.
Column 2 is the gross flow of public sector and publicly guaranteed resources.
Source: International Bank for Reconstruction and Development.

Latin American countries has been reduced, its terms, structure, and size, as compared with the value of exports, still leave much to be desired. The problem of accumulated and still rising indebtedness must be urgently and vigorously tackled both by accelerating the expansion of export earnings and by effective debt relief operations. As was stressed by the Pearson Commission, debt relief is an important form of financial co-operation that creditor countries can give, and a move in this direction could be of major importance for Latin American countries.

One step in this direction, perfectly in accordance with the trend towards multilateral development finance, would be a reconversion, through the Inter-American Development Bank and other sub-regional banks, of the outstanding Latin American debt originating from bilateral aid. By the end of 1971 this debt, excluding suppliers' credits and Export-Import Bank loans, exceeded $5,500 million. About 80 per cent of this debt was owed to the United States, which was the country that furnished Latin America with the bulk of this kind of soft financing during the 1960s.

Latin America's Outstanding Bilateral Debt
($ million)

To the U.S.A.	
AID and preceding agencies	3,500
Food for Peace Title I (payable in dollars)	300
Other loans	300
SUB-TOTAL	4,100
To Europe and Japan (est.)	1,400
TOTAL	5,500

Source · Staff work based on AID and DAC.

The bulk of this debt was contracted during the past decade as part of the Alliance for Progress programme, with grace periods averaging 10 years, and it is only in this decade that amortization quotas are falling due. According to preliminary estimates, the service on this debt during the next five years will exceed $1,000 million. Since, presumably, the United States would not wish to see net financial flows to Latin America reduced by this amount, the collection of this debt could be transferred to the Inter-American Development Bank (IDB), and possibly also, in due proportion, to the three sub-regional banks, namely, the Central American Bank for Economic Integration, the Caribbean Development Bank (CDB), and the Andean Development Corporation.

The IDB and the sub-regional banks, as the creditors for this debt, would maintain with the debtor countries the same schedule of maturities, but they could authorize programme loans up to a certain percentage of the service payments. In this way, the resources allocated to debt servicing could be channelled into development programmes.

Such a scheme would help to strengthen the Inter-American Development Bank, but other measures should also be taken to convert the Bank into an investment bank, through which the industrialized countries could extend multilateral development resources to the region.

A clear distinction should be made between concessional financing, and investment banking for development purposes; fuller participation of the industrialized countries that are not at present subscribing members of the IDB should be sought; and the Bank should develop an investment strategy in fields such as industrial development that will contribute to the expansion of trade with the industrialized countries.

The criteria for allocating concessional finance should encompass broader economic and social objectives than those associated with development investments. The IDB should separate its functions as an investment bank from its other activities, as the International Bank for Reconstruction and Development did in setting up the International Development Association to handle concessional lending and the International Finance Corporation for private sector investment. Once this is done, it would still be possible for the Board of Directors to subsidize the interest rates for ordinary development lending if prevailing international rates were considered too high for the development financing of the region.

Under the Alliance for Progress programme, evaluations of the general economic performance of countries were prepared by the Inter-American Committee on the Alliance for Progress (CIAP) and served as a guide for the allocation of concessional funds. As the inter-American system becomes more multilateral, the CIAP could fruitfully enhance its role by adding to its members the industrialized nations that participate in the IDB, and by becoming closely associated with the IDB as a body for advising on the Bank's concessional financing. CIAP could thus come to perform the kind of role that the OECD fulfils for its member countries. The past development and the present scope of the OECD would serve as a good example for a restructuring of CIAP.

Originally, the United States was the only industrialized nation to be a member of the Bank, but Canada joined in 1971. Now Japan, Germany, and other European nations are considering an invitation to subscribe 8 per cent of the enlarged capital between them. The entry of Canada and the possibility that other industrial nations may follow, is a welcome step that strengthens the institution in many ways. It puts an end to the asymmetrical position of the United States as the sole member from the industrialized world, it enlarges the resources that the Bank can lend on concessional terms, and it broadens the guarantees that the Bank can offer to subscribers to its bond issues.

The invitation to Japan, Germany, and other European nations is a move in the right direction, but it is not wholly adequate since together they are being asked to subscribe only 17 per cent of the total capital subscribed by industrialized nations.[9] The industrialized world should ideally contribute to the Bank's capital in accordance with each country's importance in the world economy and its trade and financial relations with Latin America. For example on the basis of these countries' trade with Latin America in 1970, the proportion should be more than 17 per cent: the United States should hold about 40 per cent of the capital subscribed by non-Latin American countries; nations of the enlarged European Economic Community, about 40 per cent; Japan about 10 per cent; and Canada 5 per cent.[10]

A full participation of European nations and Japan in the Bank would entail their subscribing to the Bank's ordinary capital, mainly callable capital, thus raising the ceiling for the floating of bond issues. It would also mean their contributing to the Fund for Special Operations, that is, placing funds at the disposal of the Bank for it to give credits through its soft loan window, at low rates of interest and long amortization terms. Unless present practices are changed, the contributions in soft funds would be tied to purchases in the lending country. If, however, the Bank received tied funds from many sources, none of them would be really tied, because loans could be made in the currency of the country where the borrower wished to buy.

Subscriptions of ordinary capital and contributions of concessional funds by the governments of Europe and Japan would in part replace the financing they now provide in the form of suppliers' credits, which weigh heavily on Latin America's debt service because they bear high interest rates and have relatively short periods of amortization.

The participation of Europe and Japan in the IDB and in a reorganized CIAP would also make for clearer understanding of economic and social development in the Latin American countries, and would lead to a better overall allocation of credits; this would avoid some of the causes of the repeated demands for refinancing that have occurred in the past. The reports of a reorganized CIAP would serve not only Latin American countries themselves but also those countries with which Latin America has trade and financial relations.

The Board of Directors of the IDB should include almost as many members from developed countries as from Latin American countries; their opinions, if not their votes, would carry as much weight as those of the developing countries of the region. It has been argued that this could 'de-Latinize' the institution and compel it to allocate its resources according to the priorities set forth by creditor nations and not in accordance with those of Latin America. A solution to this problem might be a two-tier system: a Board of Directors that would deal with general policies, bond issues, and the Bank's access to financial resources, and an Executive Committee of Directors, formed by Latin American members only, which would conduct the regular lending operations of the Bank.

Such far-reaching reforms could also have the desirable effect of enabling the callable capital subscribed by Latin American nations to be put to use. In theory this capital is part of the ceiling for bond issues, but in practice it is not used for this purpose, because bond issues have never exceeded the United States callable capital and, since Canada joined, the callable capital of the two countries. For both political and financial considerations, it would be advisable to include the callable capital of the Latin American countries for this purpose. From a political angle, the Latin American countries should begin to bear their share of responsibility for the Bank's operations, and from a financial angle, available lending resources would be increased to the extent that capital markets accepted these additional issues.

One way of using the Latin American callable capital as backing for the issue of additional bonds could be for the Bank to float small issues of short-term bonds with the supplementary joint guarantee of the Latin American countries. To reassure prospective subscribers the announcement should stress the fact that Argentina, Brazil, Mexico, Venezuela, and other countries that have floated several issues in various capital markets, were joint guarantors of the issue. Such Latin American guaranteed bonds should be issued only in small amounts no larger than the issues that have already been made individually by the larger Latin American countries, and devoted to specific projects of an attractive nature, and preferably of a multinational character, such as the development of regional water resources and joint hydro-electric schemes.

Additional financial resources would allow the IDB to operate as a true investment bank, supervising and co-ordinating the efforts of several financial institutions and investors. They would also enable the Bank to promote the economic integration of Latin America, and stronger trade links between the region and the industrialized member countries.

For the Bank to perform these functions more effectively the Latin American Integration Fund proposed in Chapter 7 should be set up and placed under the Bank's authority. A Latin American Finance Corporation (COFIAL) should also be established, in line with the recommendations made in 1970 by a panel of experts appointed by the Bank to discuss a report prepared by Adela.[11] Lastly, a Latin American Industrial Modernization Fund is also needed.

The Latin American Integration Fund would serve in fact as an export promotion fund, and could be used to put the region's exports on more competitive financing terms.[12] Also the Fund should finance technical assistance of the type given by the Inter-American Export Promotion Centre (CIPE) which is a valuable influence in changing the introvert national attitudes engendered by policies of import substitution towards outward-looking export promotion programmes.

COFIAL would be to a large extent the regional counterpart of the International Finance Corporation (IFC). The principal objectives of COFIAL would be to strengthen Latin American manufacturing industries through technical and financial assistance; it should be empowered to supply equity finance, as well as loans, to industrial firms, and would participate actively in the organization of new and existing enterprises. Being smaller and more specialized than the IDB itself, COFIAL should be able to assist Latin American manufacturing industries more rapidly and effectively than its parent organization, which could use it for channelling a large part of its lending to industries.

The modernization and expansion of Latin American manufacturing industries is such a formidable and important task that it justifies the creation of an Industrial Modernization Fund, which COFIAL would manage. This Fund could perhaps be the most far-reaching step in promoting Latin American integration and exports of manufactures. It would help to modernize or reconvert sectors of industry, either at the national level or among various countries, through financial and engineering programmes. These programmes would aim at orienting the future production of these industries not only to Latin American markets, but also to those of the industrialized countries.

To begin with, these industrial sectors would need to be studied in the greatest possible technical detail so that economically and politically viable arrangements could be reached with governments and representatives of domestic and foreign private industry. The resources of the Fund would then be used for financing new investments, reallocating and training the labour force that might be displaced when an industry was reorganized, and assisting the reconversion of firms that found themselves seriously affected by the readjustments.[13]

II. FOREIGN INVESTMENT IN PERSPECTIVE

Foreign direct investment in the Latin American countries does not, on the whole, appear to be greater, nor to be more involved in the economic process, than in some European countries such as Belgium, and possibly even France. It is difficult to obtain data on the relative weight of foreign capital in the countries where it is invested, but the best estimates available indicate that United States firms employ some 4 per cent of the labour force in Latin America's manufacturing industry, which compares approximately with the situation in France, where in 1970 United States companies employed 4 per cent of industrial workers. The significance of foreign private investment in Canada appears to be greater than in Latin American countries; in Canada, sales of United States subsidiary companies as a percentage of total sales was 21.8 per cent in 1964, as compared with only 7.9 per cent in Latin America.[14]

In one extremely important respect, however, Latin America differs from the countries mentioned. These have pursued rational economic policies, and foreign investment has contributed to their development and general economic progress. Even though the pay-

International Reserves, Export Earnings and Investment Income Payments of Selected Countries; Annual Averages 1967–70
($ million)

	Reserves	Export Earnings	Payments on Foreign Investment
Argentina	675	1,555	− 140
Australia	1,440	3,997	− 541
Brazil	575	2,146	− 324
Canada	3,388	16,553	− 947
Mexico	662	1,305	− 548

Source: IMF.

ments for servicing foreign investment are high, these countries have acquired a solid external financial position and have managed to accumulate large international reserves.

Canada and Australia have had high export earnings that have enabled them to service investment with ease. But Latin America's export earnings have not been adequate, with the consequence that the servicing of foreign investment has weighed heavily on the balances of payments and has impeded the accumulation of monetary reserves. In these circumstances foreign direct investment has acquired a political notoriety that has little to do with its economic defects or virtues, and has provoked between its defenders and its detractors a long and bitter polemic that is more ideological than technical.

In Latin America the political argument against foreign investment has been based largely on historical experience. Foreign capital has aroused suspicion because of interference by foreign companies, principally from the United States, in the internal political affairs of the countries where they were operating. Such interference became extensive in several countries with capital invested in sugar, bananas, and petroleum.

Another political factor that has contributed to Latin American resentment has been the support given by the governments of industrialized countries to their nationals with business in Latin America. Examples of this were the suspension by Washington of oil imports from Mexico in 1940, the intervention in Guatemala in 1954, and, more recently, the repercussions of the nationalization of the International Petroleum Company in Peru, which was more than justified by the history of that company. Such vexations have stirred up a form of nationalism that has reacted indiscriminately to all foreign investment and has frequently led to decisions that were irrational from the point of view of national economic interest.

The situation has altered considerably, however, as is clear from the example of petroleum in Venezuela. Since 1945 the government of Venezuela has used fiscal measures to obtain a progressively larger share in oil revenues, and has gradually assumed a wider role in regulating the oil industry by imposing requirements on maintenance by the companies and, in recent years, associating with other producer countries through the Organization of Petroleum Exporting Countries (OPEC). The position of the government of the United States, which is the principal investing country in Latin America, has changed, as witness its more flexible attitude towards the measures adopted by Peru and more recently by Chile. On all sides, however, this question continues to be discussed in general terms; rarely is there any attempt to identify or analyse specific cases, where widely differing conclusions may be reached, depending on the context in which the particular investment has developed.

Critics of foreign direct investment believe that foreign firms often stifle local entrepreneurial growth, distort the structure of the economy, and bring a too capital-intensive technology. The transfer of new technology, supposedly an important benefit derived from foreign direct investment, is also seen as being overpriced and sparingly given. Foreign investors are criticized for bringing little new capital into Latin America because, once they have made the initial outlay for installation, they often prefer to finance further expansion largely through reinvested earnings and local borrowing. Foreign corporations are also charged with having taken advantage of unwise Latin American import substitution regulations by setting up uneconomic industries (motor vehicles are the most striking example), where they have made large profits in a context of excessive protection.

On the investor's side there is the orthodox view that capital imports accelerate economic development by providing resources, technology, and managerial expertise. Investments create employment and provide opportunities for locally-owned enterprises to supply components. Statistics can be quoted to show how important and vigorous foreign investment is, particularly in view of the relatively small proportion of foreign to total investment.

As a rule, the argument adduced against foreign capital fails to take into account that, besides being a financial operation, foreign investment affords genuine services in technology, organization, and management, and the capacitation of human resources. All are fields that Latin America has failed to develop adequately, partly through neglect and partly through mistaken priorities. If these benefits are taken into consideration, foreign private investment has probably contributed positively to Latin America's development. This was certainly true at the end of the last and the beginning of this century when foreign investment was fundamentally involved in the development of raw materials and basic public service industries.

On the other hand, those who support foreign investment at all costs do not take into account that it has become more and more inextricably involved with an industrialization process that often has not led to viable development. The flaws of the industrialization process are, however, the responsibility of Latin American governments alone.

To the extent that an industry consists of assembly plants, and the more its products resemble imports in disguise, the more vulnerable it is.[15] From a strictly economic angle, the contribution of foreign private investment to the well-being of a nation is directly related to its allocation within the economy; the distortions produced by industrial policy, or rather absence of policy, in Latin America have not always been conducive to an optimum allocation of investment resources.[16] This does not mean, however, that all foreign capital has been badly oriented, since there are many instances, such as Volkswagen in Brazil, Olivetti in Argentina, and the *maquila* industries in Mexico, to give only three examples, of investments that are well conceived from the economic point of view, because of their adequate scale and productive organization. Also, the orientation of foreign investment in the manufacturing sector appears to be changing, and it is increasing its contribution to the growth of exports of manufactures in Brazil, Mexico, and Argentina and also in some other countries.

Within the general debate on foreign investment, there are two points that deserve special comment. Apparently, the rate of return on foreign investment in Latin America has for the most part been greater than that obtained in other areas; also foreign enterprises satisfy their financial requirements in the domestic Latin American markets through local banks to a greater extent than is usual in most other developing countries. Both problems are consequences of the countries' economic policies rather than of 'malice aforethought' on the part of the companies, which, like all enterprises that operate on the basis of maximizing profits, are prone to take advantage of any favourable state of affairs that may be offered to them. In fact, the negotiating power of any government in relation to trans-national companies is extremely broad, and even decisive if the government knows what it wants and applies policy pragmatically, case by case, as France and Mexico have done with great success.[17]

In the course of the 1970s, foreign private investment will continue to be one of the principal vehicles for importing technology into Latin America. For this reason it is important that Latin American countries choosing to use foreign investment in their development policy consider the question in a dispassionate and pragmatic manner, ignoring the ideological debate about the blessings or the blights of this investment. If there is an adequate industrial policy, and if negotiations are conducted intelligently, foreign private investment can contribute positively to the development of the Latin American economies.

Direct foreign private investment is not the only means by which Latin America can acquire technology. In general, information about the most costly aspects of technological development is not secret and is available to those who wish to avail themselves of it. If the resources devoted to research are focused on specific programmes there are many fields where Latin American countries, even acting individually, could and should finance scientific and technological development without being at a disadvantage with regard to the industrialized countries.[18]

On the other hand, technology is not nowadays derived from any particular country, but from the world in general and is constantly being exchanged between countries at what seems to be reasonable cost, possibly because the international market for technology has broadened and become more competitive.

Payments for Transfer of Technology as a Percentage of GDP

Argentina	0.72	(1969)
Brazil	0.26	(1966/68)
Colombia	0.50	(1966)
Mexico	0.76	(1968)
Chile	(0.15)	(1969)
Venezuela	(0.17)	(1969)
TOTAL LATIN AMERICA	(0.49)	

Figures in brackets are either incomplete or based on different criteria.
Source: United Nations Conference on Trade and Development, *The Transfer of Technology. Report by the Secretariat* (Geneva, 1971).

The problem would therefore seem to lie in knowing both what is available in the international market and the exact nature of the technology needed by Latin American industries. It is in general a free market and there is nothing to prevent Latin America's participating in it.

The character of foreign private investment is undergoing many changes. The diverse needs and requirements that have confronted the trans-national corporations have induced them gradually to develop a whole gamut of different devices with regard to forms of investment and participation in negotiations with foreign countries. These devices include complete participation in a negotiation, various types of association, such as association with domestic minority capital and minority participation in domestic companies, and royalty or management contracts, which even the socialist countries have been using.[19]

A promising form of participation is Adela. This is a private investment company multinationally owned, whose shareholders are large trans-national corporations established in various industrialized countries, as well as some from within Latin America. Its basic objective is to develop and encourage local private enterprise in Latin America by providing minority equity capital and medium- and long-term debt capital. Adela can give valuable assistance to export-oriented industrial development in Latin America, by sponsoring reorganizations and mergers, joint ventures, and development and modernization, both in individual countries and internationally. The Inter-American Development Bank should consider extending lines of credit to Adela to enable it to conduct such programmes on a larger scale.

At a practical level, the forms that governments allow foreign investment to assume should be chosen with flexible criteria that can be adjusted to their economic or political aims. The participation of foreign private capital is excluded from the extraction of petroleum in Brazil and from public services in other Latin American countries; it is subjected to specific regulations in various activities, as for example in the Andean Group countries, where foreign companies will not be permitted to operate in public services, banking, communications media, and certain other businesses.

The question of foreign private investment should be viewed in the context of the institutional structure that the countries decide upon, case by case. Negotiations should take advantage of the multiplicity of industrialized countries that today dispose of technologies, managerial know-how and capital that Latin America needs. There are many trans-national firms willing to negotiate from which Latin America can secure better conditions in a market where commercial competition and technical competence are increasing. In particular, the region could profit from the new phenomenon of relatively small but dynamic firms that are competing with the big corporations in the industrialized countries, and are anxious to participate more in the international market.

NOTES

[1] National corporations which operate internationally are now termed multinational, because they have profited from the financial opportunities afforded by the free movement of capital between industrialized countries. Some are becoming truly multinational within the industrialized world, and, in the case of Adela, with respect to Latin America. The issue has not yet been well defined, and it seems advisable to use the term transnational. For a discussion of multinational corporations, see *Policy Perspectives for International Trade and Economic Relations* (Paris: OECD, 1972).

[2] This question is now being discussed in the Group of Twenty, under the auspices of the International Monetary Fund. Until recently monetary affairs were discussed by the Group of Ten, but now, for the first time, developing countries are participating in these discussions in the Group of Twenty.

[3] With regard to the one per cent, which in no case is composed of net transfers, it is worth noting that the military budget of the countries of NATO and the Warsaw Pact represents about 5 per cent of their national product, which is a net waste of resources.

[4] In 1970 official development assistance represented only 0.35 per cent of the g.n.p. of those industrialized countries that were committed to giving it (compared with the UNCTAD goal of 0.7 per cent first proposed by the Pearson Commission). The OECD definition of official development assistance includes net resource transfers through multilateral institutions, and bilateral aid in the form of grants, loans repayable in the recipients' currencies, and official lending. Official lending includes loans made by governments and official agencies of more than one year's maturity, repayable in convertible currencies or in kind; official re-financing of some private loans; and small miscellaneous resource transfers. The net figure is obtained by subtracting amortization, but not interest, from gross flows.

[5] See recent studies by the Inter-American Development Bank, the Inter-American Economic and Social Council, the World Bank, and the International Monetary Fund (1971).

[6] Total external public debt at the end of 1970 can be estimated at about $20,000 million, so that the increase during the decade amounted to about $13,400 million. When grants are added, the total transfer of resources amounts to $15,000 million.

[7] These countries are Argentina, Brazil, Chile, Colombia, Mexico, and Peru.

[8] Public debt has to be serviced in order to maintain national creditworthiness. When a country is experiencing balance-of-payments problems, it can ask that remittances on foreign private investment be postponed, and this is usually agreed to.

[9] According to the projected new financial structure, Latin American members (including Jamaica, Trinidad and Tobago, and Barbados) would hold 53.5 per cent of the capital, the United States 34.5 per cent, Canada 4 per cent, and all other industrial nations 8 per cent among them. This 8 per cent amounts to 17 per cent of the capital subscribed by developed countries.

[10] Smaller proportions of total capital, since Latin American countries should maintain more than 50 per cent.

[11] The members of the panel were Walter K. Davies, Nuno F. de Figueiredo, Eduardo Figueroa, Harry Fitzgibbons, Enrique Iglesias, William R. Joyce, Adalbert Krieger Vasena, Gustavo Martínez Cabañas, and Germánico Salgado.

[12] The 'dollar shortage' of the 1950s prompted the Marshall Plan to give Europe a fund of $500 million to finance trade. The dollar shortage has long since disappeared, but the Latin American countries confront a 'foreign exchange shortage' that limits the effective financing of exports.

[13] See the experience in Europe of the European Coal and Steel Community and the European Investment Bank.

[14] See Raymond Vernon, *Sovereignty at Bay* (London: Longman, 1971); Herbert May, *The Effects of United States and other Foreign Investments in Latin America* (New York: Council of the Americas, 1969); and *Le Figaro* of 16 March 1972.

[15] It has been observed that in the case of recent nationalizations in Chile, some foreign car assembly plants, such as Ford, have been unable to make an international case against the government's decision to shut them down.

[16] Carlos Díaz Alejandro, *Direct Foreign Investment in Latin America* (New Haven, Conn.: Yale University Economic Growth Center, Paper No. 150, 1970), pp. 325–7.

[17] 'For even the biggest of the corporations in today's international political environment are in no position to seriously challenge governmental powers over monetary, fiscal, and foreign exchange matters'. Roberto Campos, *Leading Issues in Latin American Economic Development* (Speech to the Plenary Meeting of the Society for International Development, 7 March 1968).

[18] 'One extraordinary study covering the origins of five major United States innovations during the 1950s shows that the universities accounted for three quarters of the scientific events that laid the basis for industrial innovations and that half of these events occurred outside the United States'. Raymond Vernon, *Sovereignty at Bay*, p. 91.

[19] British, French, German, and Italian companies have received contracts from the Soviet Union and other East European countries to install complete plants. More recently United States corporations too have been discussing deals of this sort with the USSR and other socialist countries.

Chapter 11

A Bigger Share of World Trade

THE CENTRAL PROBLEM of Latin America's international economic relations is the steady decline of the region's share of world trade. A vigorous expansion of external trade is indispensable, not only for achieving faster economic growth, but also for setting financial transactions with the industrialized countries on a sound footing and increasing the region's self-reliance and bargain-power in the world economy.

Today, when the sharply defined economic, political, and ideological stances of the immediate post-war period are fading away, dependence has become an elusive concept, while common-sense has revealed two incontestable facts. First, if necessary imports of goods and services are paid for out of export income, whether the industries from which it originates are under domestic or foreign ownership, there are fewer constraints on the conduct of a country's internal policy than if it relies heavily on public or publicly guaranteed external finance from the industrialized countries. Second, as was discovered pragmatically in smaller countries such as Italy, Spain, or Sweden, with market economies, or Romania and Yugoslavia, with centrally planned economies, a larger and more diversified participation in world trade is the principal means of increasing a country's international freedom of action.

Export indicators for 1971

	Percentage of world exports	Exports per capita ($)	Exports as percentage of GDP
Italy	4.8	280	15.0
Sweden	2.3	588	21.0
Australia	1.6	643	14.1
Argentina	0.5	74	7.0 (1969)
Brazil	0.9	30	6.1 (1970)
Mexico	0.4	30	4.1

Source: IMF, *International Financial Statistics*.

Latin America is still very far from having devised and implemented a common international trade strategy as the EEC has
done, though CECLA was created for that purpose as long ago
as 1963. Nor can the region expect to be considered of major interest in the industrialized countries, when its trade with West
Germany is less than Austria's, when Japan trades more with
Australia and New Zealand than with Latin America, and Britain
buys more from the Scandinavian countries than from Latin
America. Economic bargaining power, in the international context,
is closely related to a country's or a region's participation in world
trade; in this respect, Italy (with five times the exports of Brazil)
or Canada (with almost twice the exports of the whole of Latin
America) is that much stronger.

Latin America's Share in the Imports of Selected Countries 1972
(percentages)

	Latin America	Argentina	Brazil	Mexico
Britain	3.1	0.7	0.8	0.1
Germany	4.1	0.7	1.1	0.1
Italy	4.2	1.4	1.3	0.2
Japan	5.3	0.3	1.1	0.9

Source: IMF, *Direction of Trade.*

The present situation has arisen partly because of inward-
looking development strategies, and partly because of a sense of
insecurity as to the region's economic capacity, which originated
with the Depression. During the past 25 years this attitude has
been reinforced by the consequent neglect of Latin America's
international trade. Problems have been tackled superficially and
some of the positive lines of action that were initiated were not
pursued with the necessary perseverance. Like its development
strategy, Latin America's trade policies have been concerned with
subordinate issues, at the expense of the primary.

Latin America has, for example, paid far too little attention to
exports of foodstuffs in the past two decades. These have not been
diversified to include items such as citrus fruits and vegetables;
nor have traditional lines, such as grain and other food products,
the demand for which has been growing steadily, been adequately
expanded.[1]

Though the problems confronting tropical food products such as
coffee and sugar in world markets account for some of the ground
lost by Latin America in world exports of foodstuffs, the feeble
effort made by the region has also contributed to its share of these

exports dropping from 25 per cent in 1950 to less than 13 per cent in 1971. In the same period, the proportion of exports originating in the industrialized countries rose from 42 to over 63 per cent. Latin America's exports of foodstuffs have been increasing by about 2.5 per cent a year, while those of the industrialized countries have grown at a rate of over 7 per cent.

Many opportunities have been lost. At the time when the European Economic Community came into being, Latin America could have negotiated broader access to the Community's market, but the region did not imagine that the EEC would materialize as a powerful bloc, and in any case Latin America had no organization at the time to represent it in general negotiations. Though LAFTA has been in existence since 1960, its secretariat has not attempted to establish common trade strategies towards other regions, and CECLA has until recently concentrated its attention mainly on establishing Latin American positions in UNCTAD.

Particularly revealing of the erroneous way in which Latin America has tackled the problems of international trade during the past ten years have been the great efforts applied to struggling for a system of generalized preferences for exports of manufactures to the industrialized countries. For Latin America, the problem has not been to gain access for its manufactures to the markets of the industrialized countries, but to produce manufactures that it could export. In fact, the markets for manufactures in the industrialized countries were so accessible that Italy, Japan, and four South-East Asian countries, were able to capture a substantial share of the United States market for goods such as textiles, transistors, plastics, and other consumer goods.

Latin America has quite enough capacity to participate more in the world economy. Examples abound, though unfortunately they are as yet isolated, of what the Latin American countries can achieve in the field of international trade, when they act efficiently and negotiate sensibly. For instance Chile, through the mechanism of LAFTA, increased her intra-regional exports, basically of pulp and paper, by 110 per cent in the short period between 1966 and 1970; Peru raised her exports of fishmeal by more than 50 per cent on the basis of an industry developed by domestic companies; Mexico used foreign investment to penetrate the United States market, and increased her exports of manufactures to that country from $20 million in 1967 to over $180 million in 1970; Argentina was able to increase her exports of manufactures from $93 million in 1966 to $243 million in 1969; and Brazil raised her exports of manufactures both to Latin America and to other markets from $400 million in 1968 to more than $800 million in 1971.

For Latin America substantially to increase its exports it will need to use the most effective mechanisms for defending the position of its traditional primary products in world markets, and to devise means of gaining access to markets for manufactures, especially in the industrialized countries. Latin America's specific trade problems vary from one group of industrialized countries to another, and it should begin to confront them in a more realistic way than it has done up to now. For this, it is indispensable that Latin America identify the central problems to be resolved with each region, so as to determine the negotiating tactics it should adopt.

I. THE PRESENT CONTEXT OF TRADE NEGOTIATIONS

The General Agreement on Tariffs and Trade (GATT) did not include some of the more substantive chapters of the Havana Charter, such as those on restrictive business practices and on inter-governmental commodity agreements. The GATT excluded most of the Charter's provisions for organization and procedure and, because of these omissions, it has not been an adequate instrument for settling the issues surrounding trade in primary products, which greatly affect the developing countries, and now even the United States, in their trade with Europe.

The GATT has tended to assume the role of regulatory body in the expansion of trade in manufactures between the industrialized countries. The progress recorded in the liberalization of world trade in manufactured products contrasts noticeably with the minor advance, and in some cases the regression, that has occurred in the trading conditions for most primary products. The failure of the Kennedy Round in 1967 to tackle the burning issue of primary (especially agricultural) products, demonstrated the refusal of the industrialized countries to modify their restrictive policies.

In response to this situation, the developing countries created the United Nations Conference on Trade and Development (UNCTAD), in which Latin America has participated with enthusiasm; like the immediate post-war trade discussions that culminated in the Havana Conference, UNCTAD offered an opportunity to approach problems of international trade at a global level, over the heads of groups or blocs of countries.[2] Indeed, in the course of the past five years, some advances have been made through this means of negotiation.

Among the most important steps have been the negotiation of several commodity agreements between consumer and producing countries. Also, within the GATT, a system of non-reciprocal generalized preferences has been accepted and in part put into effect, with some benefit to exports of manufactures from the developing countries. UNCTAD undoubtedly has a role to play in improving the flow of international trade, and Latin America can join in this to its advantage. It is important, however, that Latin America realize the limitations of UNCTAD and, through political action within the organization, attempt to concentrate the energies of this potentially important United Nations body on aspects of the restructuring of world trade that it can most effectively influence.

There are at present several important technical tasks that UNCTAD could perform at the policy level, which would certainly take up all its energies. One of these would be to assure that the interests of developing countries are fully taken into consideration in the successive trade negotiations in GATT. Another would be to seek solutions to the clash of interests between Latin America and other developing regions consequent on the creation by the EEC of a very large preferential area. This arrangement which with Britain's entry can include as many as 50, mostly developing, countries is strongly opposed by both the United States and Japan and seems likely to be detrimental to Latin America's trade with Europe.

UNCTAD could also devise formulas for a substantial expansion of trade among the developing countries, which now represents less than 4 per cent of world trade. Though developing countries compete for international trade in primary products, their divergent levels of development could well enable them to increase their commercial interchanges. For example, Latin American and African nations could attempt imaginative types of arrangement serving the interests of both. A Latin American country might relinquish the export of a certain amount of primary products to the industrialized countries in return for an African country's granting the Latin American country preferential treatment for manufactured imports. The industrialized countries, for their part, would lose markets for manufactures in Africa, but would gain markets for capital goods in Latin America.[3]

For the time being, this is perhaps the most that UNCTAD can achieve for Latin America, which has trade problems of a very special nature. As UNCTAD III demonstrated, the member countries and the economic subjects have become so numerous that these meetings have lost much of their effectiveness; only very general plans can be considered, and no concrete international negotiations can be conducted.[4]

II. A NEW APPROACH TO THE INDUSTRIALIZED COUNTRIES

Latin America's basic political challenge at present is to become more interdependent with the industrialized countries. To achieve this, the region needs to put an end to 'external insufficiency' and 'financial dependence' by expanding its trade with those countries, which basically means substantially increasing exports of manufactured goods to them.

A minor first international step in the right direction has already been taken. Twelve industrialized countries have already established a non-reciprocal system of generalized preferences in favour of the developing countries. This is not, however, the panacea that it was held to be in Latin America. The system excludes numerous products, subjects some imports to quotas, and is hemmed in by numerous safeguard clauses. It is estimated that by the mid-1970s the additional volume of exports that these preferences will stimulate will be worth only $300 million a year. And this only when the United States grants them too.[5]

Given the magnitude of the economic and social problems of the developing countries, these concessions in the commercial arena are minimal. It is instructive to consider the volume of international trade that could have been created if the developed countries had been importing the manufactures that they are now producing domestically with labour drawn from relatively less developed regions. Had the developing nations been exporting these goods, instead of merely exporting the labour to produce them, the impact on their economies would have been resounding. Estimates indicate that the Turkish, Greek, and Yugoslav workers in West Germany's manufacturing industry alone, are generating a gross value of production that, had it been in the form of West German imports of manufactures, would have been equivalent to more than half the value of Latin America's total exports.

The reluctance of the industrialized countries to contribute to improving trade conditions in a shrinking world is explained, in large measure, by the inadequacies of their own economic policies. They have allowed the emergence of social predicaments and economic trends that are seriously impeding their growth and their capacity to adjust their external sectors to the changing pattern of a world economy for which they are themselves largely responsible.

The industrialized countries have neglected policies for improving personal and regional income distribution; as a result of social pressures and regional imbalance, inflation and unemployment have ensued. This sequence is generating a kind of national introspection and a lack of concern for the problems of the world economy, and impeding the solution of the grave problems that beset all countries' international economic relations.

A more determined approach to these problems by the industrialized countries would not only be to their own advantage but would also benefit the developing world and Latin America. It would open up genuine trade possibilities for industrialized and developing countries alike and would promote economic advancement more effectively than 'aid', 'preferences', or 'technical assistance' on the scale and in the form that they are now conceived.

Planning has been enthusiastically commended for the developing nations, but where it is really needed, and should be fulfilling an important role, is in the industrialized countries, which will be unable to maintain adequate growth rates without, for example, being obliged to continue to import manpower to work in low-productivity industries; they should bear constantly in mind the need to convert production towards more productive technologies and activities, while eliminating lower productivity industries, such as textiles. It would be profitable for the international bodies and the governments of the industrialized countries to undertake comprehensive industrial planning, and the gradual conversion of certain industries.

The urgency of these questions for the industrialized countries is greater than is often admitted. Growth based on overpriced agriculture and defective industrialization, or maintained by the immigration of cheap labour, will produce far-reaching social conflicts.[6] These will be compounded by restrictions derived from environmental considerations in overpopulated and heavily industrialized areas, where, until very recently, little was being done to cope with these problems.[7] Other steps that these countries could take would be to accelerate long-term agricultural reforms, such as those envisaged for the EEC, by the Mansholt Plan, and the setting-up of industrial reconversion funds similar to those of the European Coal and Steel Community (ECSC), which enabled the EEC countries to run down an inefficient coalmining industry, and to begin importing coal at much lower prices. In the EEC countries a reduction of the subsidies to agriculture would free resources that would be more than enough to finance the industrial reconversion funds.[8] The same would be true in the United States with the elimination of agricultural products such as sugar beet that are, directly or indirectly, heavily subsidized.

Latin America, with an industrial structure that already generates numerous external economies, with an underemployed labour force, and a very low level of environmental contamination, should earnestly consider how it can take advantage of this situation. Latin American policy-makers should begin to study, and to negotiate in the industrialized countries, with trans-national corporations in the West, and with state enterprises in the socialist countries, major forms of international co-operation aimed at increasing Latin American exports of industrial products.

There is currently some opposition to the exporting of industries, in Europe because of fears that the developing countries cannot guarantee regular supplies, and in the United States because of the resistance of organized labour to the 'exporting of jobs'; nevertheless, this will be the future trend. The big trans-national companies already acknowledge this and have begun to veer towards it, though in doing so they have created some suspicion and misunderstanding both in Latin America and in the industrialized countries. While in many cases Latin American firms will be able to make use of the marketing facilities of these trans-national corporations by associating with them in joint ventures, they should also themselves participate actively in the export of manufactures.

Trans-national corporations have already begun to take advantage of lower labour costs in developing countries by setting up production for export to the industrialized countries. This pattern should be encouraged, for example, through sectoral industrial complementation agreements. Means of associating Latin American firms with certain industrial processes in the industrialized countries could be negotiated at government level with the active participation of entrepreneurs from both sides. The IDB, Adela, and other regional financial institutions, could very well promote these arrangements with feasibility studies.

In this form of co-operation firms in the industrialized countries would commission from Latin American plants the manufacture of certain components, which could be of types involving a relatively advanced degree of technology, but also requiring a high level of manpower. For their part, firms in the industrialized countries would benefit from production costs, especially labour costs, noticeably lower than those prevailing in their home markets.

III. DEVISING VERSATILE COMMERCIAL POLICIES

The industrialized countries will continue for some years discussing conditions for achieving more balanced trade and financial transactions among themselves. To take full advantage of the possibilities offered by this new juncture, as well as of contradictory positions among the industrialized countries, Latin America will need to devise effective methods for negotiating its commercial relations with each of the various industrialized regions.

The European Economic Community affirms that the United States government is not as liberal in its trade policy as it claims to be, since there are restrictions in the form of quotas, 'The American Selling Price' and 'Buy American Rules'; and that it operates much stricter anti-dumping legislation than that of the European countries. The EEC appears to believe, however, that it is possible to negotiate the liberalization of world trade, always provided that the United States is prepared to make concessions.

The position of the EEC on United States trade policy coincides with that of Latin America, which is already, but not very effectively, negotiating through the Special Committee for Co-ordination and Negotiation (CECON) on the non-tariff barriers applied by the United States to many of the region's exports.

Washington has for many years followed the practice of fixing quotas and other open or disguised quantitative restrictions on certain imports, which have contributed to the worsening of Latin America's trade balances with the United States. As long as conditions in the United States market continue to prevent Latin American exports from expanding faster, the growing deficit on current account will compel Latin American countries to increase imports from those areas with which they have trade surpluses, so as to stimulate the growth of exports to those markets at an even faster pace.

While Latin America's views on United States trade restrictions coincide broadly with those of Europe, the converse is also true. The United States has been insisting that her trade deficit stems from the other industrialized countries' thwarting an increase in the volume of American exports by the use of trade restrictions and the undervaluation of their currencies. Washington also maintains that high internal prices and the system of levies are provoking agricultural overproduction in Europe, and the supplanting of cheaper foodstuffs from the United States; this position on the opening-up of Europe for imports of food products suits Latin America's commercial interests. The agricultural policy of the enlarged European Community, as well as its policy of association for ex-colonial developing countries, limits its imports of food products from Latin America no less than from the United States. Europe's discrimination in favour of such a broad bloc of developing countries presents Latin America with the question of whether to sound out the other industrialized countries on establishing a system of reciprocal preferences.

During the present phase of monetary and commercial readjustment among the major trading powers, Latin America could again become a significant region for those economies that since the war have evolved more openly than that of the United States, and whose economic success was partly a cause of the recent United States suspension of dollar convertibility. This is a possibility that Latin America should consider actively. The region should strive to intensify its trade relations with Japan, Germany, Italy, Canada, Australia, and Yugoslavia, for example; also, now that China and the Comecon countries are rapidly expanding their trade with the Western world, an excellent opportunity is opening up for Latin American trade with them.

Japan in particular will need to diversify her commercial relations, so as to be less dependent on the United States market, and indeed, is already exploring trade possibilities with the Soviet Union. Japan presents two further advantages in connection with expanding commercial relations with Latin America. First, to maintain a high rate of savings and economic expansion Japan earlier imposed restrictions on the consumption of foodstuffs, including meat and tropical products such as coffee, through a stringent system of quantitative import controls. With the level of incomes now attained, Japan is under pressure to liberalize imports. Latin America could become a major supplier of agricultural requirements to Japan, and could increase its imports from Japan commensurately.

Second, Japan appears to be one of the few industrialized countries that has taken the trouble to programme and direct its industrial policy. Thus, just as Sweden closed down her textile industry on account of the high opportunity cost of employing manpower in this sector, Japan has begun to export to neighbouring countries, such as Taiwan and Korea, industries designed to supply the Japanese market. The transfer of this kind of industry to Latin America ought to be one of the central points in high-level negotiations between Japan and Latin America.

Trade with the socialist countries is a good example of how the problems confronting Latin America differ from one area to another. As is underlined in Chapter 9, the expansion of the region's trade with Comecon countries runs up against accumulated trade surpluses in favour of Latin America. Negotiations between the Latin American and the Soviet bloc countries should be directed to setting up multilateral arrangements for clearing through third parties the credits that Latin America accumulates in the Comecon group. These countries are now expanding their trade and financial relations with Europe, the United States, and Japan; credit balances with these trading partners could be cleared against the debit balances in favour of Latin America; the region would thus acquire purchasing power in the West. Furthermore, the establishment of trans-national companies in the socialist countries, with the purpose of benefiting from lower wages and exporting to third countries, will provide more acceptable goods to trade with Latin America, as well as trilateral trade opportunities that could be arranged through these companies.

In the decades to come, Latin America will be presented with increasing opportunities in international trade. In particular, the protracted negotiations among the major powers on restructuring the world trade and monetary machinery could profoundly affect the region. To take part in and benefit from the changes that are occurring, Latin America needs to revise its development strategy and organize itself so as to participate effectively in negotiations, and obtain better conditions for expanding its trade with the industrialized world. Through an organization such as CECLA, which is thoroughly responsive to the interests of Latin America and is competent to co-ordinate them into a unified thesis, the region can establish the appropriate negotiating machinery.

NOTES

[1] Argentina, for example, unlike Canada, has not pursued a policy of stockpiling her wheat so as to sell it at opportune moments.

[2] The first Secretary General of UNCTAD was a Latin American, Raúl Prebisch, who vigorously called the attention of the developed world to these crucial matters.

[3] These types of arrangement have been suggested by Santiago Macario.

[4] For a study of UNCTAD's achievements up to the end of the third conference in Santiago in April-May 1972, see Lloyds & Bolsa International Bank, 'The Lessons of UNCTAD III', *Bolsa Review*, November 1972.

[5] *The Economist*, 18 March 1972, p. 72.

[6] In the countries of the enlarged European Economic Community there are at present 7 million foreign workers, not counting the Italians in a country such as Germany, who have freer access because Italy is a member of the Community. For a discussion of this point, see C. L. Sulzberger, 'Second Class Citizens in Developed Countries', *New York Times*, 9 June 1972, p. 37.

[7] See Donella H. Meadows *et al.*, *The Limits to Growth: A Report for the Club of Rome's Project on the Predicament of Mankind* (New York: Universe Books, for Potomac Associates, 1972).

[8] See the section on trade policies in Chapter 8.

Chapter 12

Meeting the Challenge

LATIN AMERICA IS faced with the challenge of making up for the time that it has lost in the past 25 years. The region has failed to develop faster and to participate more in the world economy because it has not made full use of the advantages that its semi-development offers. Chastened by the sharp reduction in trade during the Depression and the Second World War, the countries of the region sought a greater degree of self-sufficiency and adopted inward-looking development strategies as described in Chapter 2. Though soon after the war such policies ceased to be necessary, they were continued for the sake of short-term political objectives.[1]

The most far-reaching effect of the Latin American countries' singleminded pursuit of development strategies based on import substitution has been their failure to construct an industrialization policy capable of providing the region with efficient and competitive industries. This deficiency has harmed the Latin American countries in several ways : it has consolidated a pattern of inequitable income distribution; it has made economies progressively more awkward to manage, because of distortions in the market system arising from excessive protection; and, worst of all, it has prevented Latin America from participating in the exceptional post-war boom in world trade, largely concentrated in manufactured goods, and has compelled the external sector of the Latin American economies to continue to rely heavily on primary commodities. Attempts have been made to remedy the situation through economic planning, but the results have been modest because there has been no fundamental revision of development strategy, least of all in the sphere of industrialization.

Such a revision is difficult to carry out; not only has Latin America squandered a great deal of time, but it has done so in a way that obstructs a change of course. A structure of vested interest has been firmly established around these policies of import substitution at any cost, while the region's poor external per-

formance has inculcated in it a sense of insecurity, especially regarding its capacity to participate in the international economy.
This insecurity is found on both the Right and the Left, among
fainthearted Latin Americans who are afraid of change, whether in
the shape of competition in international trade, modern technology,
foreign capital, or the political implications of trading with
socialist countries.

A dangerous symptom of this fear is all the current theorizing
on 'dependence', which leads to the erroneous conclusion that
little or nothing can be done in Latin America if the 'perverse
world' does not change. The region has not learned the lesson
demonstrated by countries such as Canada, Australia, and some
of the smaller nations of western Europe, such as Sweden
and Belgium, which have had to contend with circumstances
similar to those of Latin America. For these countries the achievement of successful economic development has called for a high
degree of external interchange or interdependence. Latin America
has no viable alternative but to follow this example. If it does not
actively negotiate with the industrialized countries for an expansion
of trade flows, investment and financial transactions, and the exchange of technology and know-how, it will only reinforce its
dependence.

Yet Latin America appears, in general, to have opted for
ideology rather than the pragmatism that prevails in the
industrialized countries and explains much, from the industrialization of the Soviet Union to the economic success of the European
Economic Community. The responsibility lies squarely with those
leaders who have selected the wrong objectives, evinced lack of
vision, and been wanting in the tenacity to follow up initiatives
such as integration.

If Latin American governments give way to fear or ideological
aberrations, they will be unable to fulfil the aspirations and
material needs of the people; concern over such problems should
be balanced by an appreciation of the region's achievements and
potential. Latin America is well endowed with the resources
necessary to achieve greater technological capacity and a larger
share in world trade. What is required is the political determination to organize these resources in the right direction.

If the region is not to be left on the sidelines of the international economy, it will have to act promptly, for decisions made
in the next few years will probably shape the world economic
system for the rest of the century. A reordering of the international
monetary system has been made subject to negotiation on the
conditions governing the conduct of international trade. The scope

of the negotiations that are now being prepared goes beyond a straight confrontation between the United States and the EEC, and must eventually include other OECD countries and the Comecon bloc.

Latin America can ill afford to stand aloof from the complete realignment of a world that is becoming more and more interconnected in every respect. However, the countries of the region find themselves ill-prepared and poorly equipped to participate in a world where the external autonomy of a country is determined by the strength of its economy and its capacity to influence collective decision-making. To illustrate this point, the imports of even the largest Latin American countries, Argentina, Brazil, and Mexico, currently account for only 0.56, 1.0, and 0.61 per cent respectively of the world total, compared with 5 per cent each for Canada and Italy.

To acquire adequate international economic bargaining power, the Latin American countries will need, not only to forge ahead with development, but also to strengthen their regional cooperation. Until Latin America presents greater unity in facing other countries, its hand in international negotiations will be very weak. It is utterly unrealistic to suppose that an amorphous group of countries will even be heard in a world where Europe has been compelled to speak more and more as one unit in order to negotiate effectively with the other industrialized blocs. As the European example demonstrates, successful economic integration is an important prerequisite to establishing the community of interests required for a unified approach to other nations or blocs. Latin America, too, should organize its external negotiating capacity around the economic integration process.

I. INTEGRATION

Despite the resolution made at the summit meeting of the Presidents of Latin America and the United States in 1967, a Latin American Common Market did not begin to come into existence in 1970. Moreover, the possibility of achieving a fully operative common market by 1985 has receded; not only has the date for initiating it been postponed, but also a tendency towards dispersal into sub-groups has appeared. The Andean Group has been set up partly in response to the slow progress of LAFTA, and partly to meet a political desire to establish a better balance of forces within LAFTA. This move, and the stalemate in which LAFTA finds itself, could in turn lead to other groupings, which

F

in the long run would only weaken Latin American unity still more, and further reduce the region's significance in the balance sheet of the world economy. For example, there is ample geographic and economic justification for extending to a full integration agreement the River Plate Basin agreement for the joint development of the resources of the Paraná system.

To counteract these tendencies, Latin America needs to take practical steps to revitalize economic integration. Most effective would be the granting of preferences by the larger countries to the small and medium countries. An examination of the structure of intra-Latin American trade, both between countries and by types of products, throws into relief the predominance of the big three – Argentina, Brazil, and Mexico – in the region's trade, especially trade in manufactures. Further general liberalization would almost certainly give the larger countries even greater advantages; hence these three should give the others (including, of course, the members of the CACM and CARIFTA) preferential treatment as a means of expediting integration. This preferential treatment would help to dispel the suspicions, distrust, and apprehensions that affect negotiations between the large, medium, and small countries, each of which believes it is being harmed more than the others, though European experience clearly shows that a less industrialized country such as Italy and a more industrialized one such as Germany can benefit equally from integration.

There are good grounds for believing that such a system of intra-Latin American preferences would have the desired effect. In 1964 the LAFTA agreement was modified to allow sectoral agreements (co-ordinating two or more countries' production in a particular sector) to be excluded from the most-favoured nation clause; concessions contained in such agreements are not now automatically extended to the other signatory countries. This has afforded greater flexibility in the sectoral field than has been possible in general negotiations, and greater progress has been achieved through industrial complementation by sectors than in negotiating the national and common lists of products for liberalization.

This success reflects the apprehensions of the larger countries, each of which has been reluctant to extend to the other large economies the concessions made to the small and medium countries. The smaller countries have, for their part, been wary of extending concessions negotiated among themselves to the big three whose industrial skills, productive capacity, and market potential are more developed.

By a political decision at the highest level, the three large countries, as well as any other nation, such as Venezuela, which considered that it could open its market to the small and medium countries of the region, could grant the rest a system of concessions. The products of the small and medium countries, whether raw materials or manufactures with an authenticated certificate of origin, would be allowed to obtain rapid access – within three to five years – to the markets of the three largest countries. So that the impact of this liberalization be felt, all non-tariff barriers should be eliminated at the moment the concession is decided upon, and tariff barriers reduced to zero in the course of the three- to Mexico is very deep-seated, these concessions should not be extended among them. Furthermore, to make the scheme more attractive to these three countries, the other countries could grant them a general across-the-board preference, below present levels of protection.

After this stage, a second series of measures should be taken. The countries that have given trade concessions to the small and medium-size countries can negotiate among themselves a more gradual scheme of liberalization of their trade, which is quite feasible, since it would involve economies of a more or less equal level of industrial development. It would also permit the negotiation of concrete trade agreements, which is impossible today in so broad a negotiating forum as LAFTA. The medium and small countries of the region could also agree among themselves a separate but parallel scheme of trade liberalization. The third stage of the process would be the establishment of a common external tariff for all the countries of the region.

It is still possible today for the Latin American countries to take a political decision in favour of a course such as the one outlined, as a means of attaining rapid and effective integration. Time is running short, however, and if Latin America indeed wishes to have a voice and carry weight in the decisions that will change the system and the organization of the world economy in the years to come, it must not delay any longer taking the first steps towards setting up a Latin American common market.

II. ORGANIZING FOR THE FUTURE

There are valid precedents for joint international action by the countries of Latin America. They formed a bloc in the United Nations from the very beginning in 1946, to present a common position within that organization. The Latin American countries have always acted in unison at the annual assemblies of the International Monetary Fund and the World Bank. The three directors who represent the region on the boards of these institutions have successfully carried out their duties even when, for example, one country has been representing another whose monetary problems differed substantially from its own.

If Latin America wishes to participate more fully in the international economy, it should follow these precedents by adopting modes of international negotiation that are more competent and mature than those used by the region during the past decade through the inter-American system and UNCTAD. Integration along the lines recommended should provide, as it has done in Europe, foundations on which Latin America can construct a simple institutional framework that will allow it to negotiate effectively with others.

The granting of preferences by the larger countries would be the first in a series of essentially political measures which would strengthen the unity of Latin America, and enable it to play a broader role in the world economy. Latin America will require an organization that is capable of smoothing its path and guiding it in this process. The most important step taken towards the unification of Latin America in the past 25 years was the creation of the Special Committee for Latin American Co-ordination (CECLA). The Committee should now be established as a permanent institution; it would be the ideal instrument for devising policies to advance integration, undertaking economic negotiations with the industrialized regions and countries, and formulating valid positions on international monetary and trade problems. If it were assigned this political role, CECLA would be the appropriate body for supervising matters such as the implementation of the preferences given by the larger countries to the rest. It would also be the most suitable forum in which to discuss any additional measures that might be needed.

The Committee itself could well set up a task force to decide its new terms of reference. These would have to be approved in a conference of all the Latin American Heads of State. Once CECLA became a political forum for determining overall integration policy, LAFTA, the Andean Group, CACM, and CARIFTA would be free to concentrate on the important function of carrying out their respective agreements. This would be a division of responsibilities similar to that devised in the EEC, where the high authority of the European Coal and Steel Community, which was instrumental in the practical application of integration, was only after some years incorporated into the Executive Commission of the EEC.

The Special Committee for Consultation and Negotiation (CECON) has already been established by CECLA as a permanent body for handling economic, especially trade, matters with the United States. A reorganized CECLA should set up similar bodies to consult and negotiate regularly with the enlarged European Economic Community, with Japan, with the Comecon, and with China. Within the framework of the IMF, where Latin America has had three representatives for many years, three Latin American countries – Argentina, Brazil, and Mexico – have been designated members of the Group of Twenty, which is to negotiate world monetary reform. The present state of flux in the world economy goes deeper than the financial crisis, however, and will entail a readjustment of world trade. Latin America needs to co-ordinate its stand on these issues, and should do so through CECLA.

The way in which CECLA is reorganized should take account of its dual role as a policy forum and a negotiating body. Though CECLA would have no pretensions to supra-national powers, the realistic formula of the Council of Ministers of the EEC should be followed to some extent, in relating the weight carried by each country in CECLA to its economic importance. To ensure the competence of CECLA in trade and financial matters, the countries should be represented on the Committee by their ministers of economy.

Permanent headquarters should be installed for CECLA in Latin America, and the Committee should be equipped with a highly qualified secretariat to undertake staff work. A very important element of this work would be the technical preparation of items to be discussed in the permanent bodies that would be established for negotiating with the industrialized countries. The secretariat would also be responsible for keeping CECLA constantly informed on the course of international trade and financial negotiations. Since the Organization for Economic Co-operation and Development (OECD) will be the principal link between the deliberations of the Group of Twenty and the trade negotiations that the industrialized countries are planning to conduct within the framework of GATT, the secretariat of CECLA will need to maintain close contact with it. To facilitate the exchange of views, the secretariat of CECLA should be given permanent observer status in the OECD.

Other measures, besides the adoption of a more realistic integration policy and the reorganization of CECLA, will be needed to enable Latin America to participate fully in the world economy. The Inter-American Development Bank (IDB) should become the main financial link between Latin America and its trading partners in the industrialized countries. This will necessitate the Bank's making a very clear distinction between its functions as an investment bank and its role as a multilateral channel for financial assistance to those less-developed Latin American countries and regions that require it. As a development bank, the IDB should undertake to promote and finance economic integration and industrial expansion. For these two purposes the IDB should manage the Latin American Integration Fund and, through COFIAL, the Latin American Industrialization Fund.

Latin America would also require a multilateral consultative body to consider general economic development problems derived from external financial needs and international trade. Such a body could be formed by enlarging the Inter-American Committee on the Alliance for Progress (CIAP) to include other industrialized countries as well as the United States, and by associating it closely with the IDB, which it could advise on outlays of concessional finance. In this way, CIAP could come to serve Latin America in much the same way that the OECD usefully serves its members.

III. THIS DECADE AND BEYOND

It would be disastrous if Latin America were to choose seclusion or isolationism when an unusual juncture in international economic relations is offering it an opportunity of regaining the active participation in the world economy that it formerly enjoyed. There are Latin Americans who will claim that the region, because of its problems and the unhelpful attitudes of the developed countries, should retreat into isolationism and adopt policies of 'inwardly-directed development'. But in many respects it is this pattern of development in Latin America that during the past 25 years has caused the inadequacy of the region's external resources and brought about its dependence.

What prevents Latin America from breaking out of this pattern is not any lack of internal potential, which is ample, nor the external impediments, which are manageable, but the lack of will among Latin American leaders to apply the potential at their disposal so as to improve the lot of the Latin American people. Regardless of the socio-political system it chooses, each country should concentrate on the primordial task of using its human and natural resources diligently and effectively. Only by increasing the production of goods and services at the highest possible rate, can the Latin American countries provide their citizens with the decent level of material welfare to which they aspire. To divert attention from this crucial problem, as has been done, is sheer irresponsibility on the part of leaders.

The Latin Americans have no reason to set their sights low. The region can perfectly well close the gap between semi-development and full development in the next thirty years. Latin Americans would be wise, however, to take account of the social problems that today face the industrialized countries; economic growth may be an indispensable condition, but it will not alone ensure the attainment of acceptable forms of social existence.

A serious and rational endeavour to direct and expand productive capacity could endow the region with the economic basis for imaginative forms of social existence of an intrinsically Latin American character. This endeavour would also result in Latin America's again assuming a position of world stature, as it did in the nineteenth century when it achieved its political independence.

NOTES

[1] One outstanding exception is Brazil, where over the past decade the inward-looking development strategy has been in some measure reoriented.

[2] For the views of Pierre Uri and John Tuthill on the possible merits of sub-regional groups, see below, p. 190.

Comments by Members of the Steering Committee

Víctor L. Urquidi,
Chairman of the Steering Committee

AS CHAIRMAN OF THE STEERING COMMITTEE set up for this study, I find myself in an uncomfortable situation. The purpose of the Steering Committee was to provide guidance to the authors of the study and to comment on early drafts of the report. This was done on at least three occasions, and, as Chairman, I had several additional opportunities to comment on parts of the report and two earlier drafts with the authors. It was agreed, however, that only they would bear responsibility for the final text and recommendations. The purpose of this comment is to clarify my position on certain portions of the report, particularly the interpretation and analysis of Latin America's development problems, but also on a few of the conclusions and recommendations.

I do not wish to detract, however, from the high quality of the work performed by Dr Krieger Vasena and Mr Pazos, and their assistants. They have drawn attention to serious problems facing the Latin American countries in their present and future economic and financial relations with the industrialized countries, and they have also brought to the fore certain basic problems of development and integration. I am able to support their broad thesis that Latin America must regain the time lost and participate in the expansion of world trade in manufactured products, and must consequently make its industry and other activities more efficient and competitive at the same time that it improves its organization for negotiating multilaterally with the world trade blocs. Many of the specific proposals on external debt and financing, foreign private investment, reallocation of industry from developed to less developed countries, and Latin American integration, are eminently sensible and should be carefully considered by the interested governments and other groups. But I do not share the authors' views on the broader framework of Latin American societies and the ultimate objectives of development, and I find it necessary to make the following brief statements.

1. Latin America is not today what it is because of the influence of 'ideology', 'irrational behaviour' of politicians and technocrats, the 'simplistic' doctrines of economists associated with the Economic Commission for Latin America, or of sociologists who have drawn attention to the high complexity of development under conditions of dependence. Latin American problems have deep historical origins. There is great diversity in Latin America, not only in historical experience, but also in approaches to the solution of development problems. Even in countries where a certain amount of social reform has taken place under pressure from rural or urban groups, or from reform-minded politicians or intellectuals, the forces opposing change – connected with traditional or newly-formed landed interests, industry, commerce, and finance, usually allied with foreign investors – have been strong enough to prevent significant reductions in inequality and injustice, privilege and backwardness, under the general patterns of economic growth. Some of the countries showing the highest rates of economic expansion, even under so-called revolutionary governments, are also those where old inequalities have remained and possibly even been intensified. Surely success in development must be measured not only by industrial production and participation in world markets, but also by redressment of social imbalances and improvement in the material and cultural conditions of the rural and urban working population. In my view, not enough emphasis is given by the authors to this necessary process – the interaction of social and economic development – nor to the structural factors connected with landownership, concentration of industrial property, the lack of educational opportunity, and similar basic aspects of society. A prescription of more 'production' and 'efficiency', contained throughout the report, will fall far short of creating a just society in Latin America and will reduce its capacity ultimately to perform precisely the active role in world affairs that the authors recommend. Inequality and structural distortions will not disappear merely by following 'pragmatic' approaches to increasing agricultural and industrial output. An integrated socio-economic view is indispensable for laying out a long-run strategy of development and trade. Three or four Latin American countries – hardly mentioned by the authors – are attempting it.

2. It follows that the economic solutions prescribed by the authors for Latin America's trade and financial problems cannot be dealt with in isolation, i.e., independently of what happens in other less developed areas. There is good reason to urge those

countries that are better developed to take advantage of possibilities of negotiation and assume leadership in their own interest and that of the region. But it is not a question of Latin America 'joining the club' – be it the European Economic Community or some North Atlantic-Japanese trade association. Despite the 'semi-development' adduced by the authors (incidentally, not strictly defined or substantiated), Latin America by and large forms part of the Third World and must share the aspirations of this part of the world for a better international economic order in which the developed countries carry out their responsibilities to the less developed parts of humanity whose weaknesses have been so much abused economically and politically. For this reason, I cannot agree that Latin America should dissociate itself from the 'confrontation' that takes place under UNCTAD, and this in spite of differences with certain African and Asian countries. The Third World countries as a whole have considerable leverage that has not been adequately used, and much can be learned by Latin America from the experience of similar areas, and vice versa. Moreover, it is not realistic to assume that international negotiations on trade, finance, technology, and investment will take place in a political vacuum, subject only to 'pragmatic' and 'rational' policies of 'business-minded' people. Too much is at stake for Latin America to assume that structural changes can be a direct result of the expansion of manufactured exports to the wealthy countries without a revision of the international rules of the game.

3. In spite of their carefully worded paragraphs on Latin America's population problem and their taking account of diverse conditions in different countries, in my opinion the authors underestimate the negative significance of the high rates of population growth prevailing in most of the region. In turn, they overestimate the importance of territory and potentially usable land in certain countries and seem to think that a 'reverse migration' from urban to rural areas is possible. Those points were argued extensively with the authors in the earlier drafts and I therefore wish to record my differences with respect to their analysis and outlook. In my view, positive policies to reduce the rate of population growth through active programmes to lower fertility are necessary and urgent as an aid in the development process – the sooner the better. Let there be no illusion about the ability of the Latin American countries to cope with 20 to 25 years' population doubling times, in economic, social, or political terms. In a dynamic analysis, taking all factors into consideration, population 'density' is a clearly inadequate concept. The special case of Argentina should not be generalized to the whole region, and even that

country has differential fertility rates that contribute to its social and economic problems in areas of high urban concentration. It is strange that a report which puts so much emphasis on productivity should seem to imply that high productivity is related to high population growth rather than to capital formation and a better use of technology. The employment implications of high population growth are hardly touched upon. Contrary to the authors' view, part of the answer to the employment problem lies in a reduction of fertility.

4. In my view, the authors overrate the benefits to be derived from foreign private investment in Latin America and minimize the extent of political influence by trans-national and other foreign corporations. The Andean investment code – not mentioned in the report – and similar policies followed and measures taken in other countries in the region are evidence that political factors cannot be dissociated from the problem of foreign investment and that the role of foreign direct investment must be complementary to national effort and fit in with national political and development objectives. The abuses of foreign corporations are many and have to do with licensing agreements, restrictive practices, overpricing of imports of equipment and materials, and many similar features recently analysed in the literature and from case studies. To ignore these factors is hardly realistic. In addition, there has been political interference and, generally, association with the local forces that accept the established system and view of development. While foreign private corporations may not be able to behave much differently, it is the responsibility of Latin American governments to develop national policies to deal with foreign participation in development, in order to benefit from the technological and financial inputs without their implying domination of domestic economic policy. This is the single most important problem affecting relations between Latin America and the industrial countries, and should be carefully considered in any expansion of relations with Europe, Canada, and Japan.

5. Since the final draft of the report is given as definitive, it would not be possible to suggest to the authors reconsideration of certain passages. Nor would it be practical to mention every small point of discrepancy. I shall limit myself to a few points which seem important to me : (a) I have doubts as to the advisability and feasibility of a one-way trade preference on the part of Argentina, Brazil, and Mexico, to the other countries in Latin America, be they LAFTA, Andean Pact, or other; I am in favour of across-the-board efforts on as wide a geographical basis as possible, as an

aid to Latin American economic integration. Incidentally the analogy between the EEC and LAFTA to argue that planning of integration aspects is not necessary, is a false one. (b) I cannot agree to the suggestion that Spain – or any other non-Latin American country – should become an associated member of LAFTA or the CACM. It is neither economically logical nor politically acceptable. (c) How can Australia and New Zealand be 'natural partners' for Latin America? A geographical criterion is not necessarily an economic one. (d) Latin America is not faced with a choice between increasing output for export and obtaining preferential treatment, but should be able to accomplish both objectives. (e) The alleged attitude of expecting 'outside sources' to resolve Latin America's problems is far from universal in the region; on the contrary, there is a growing determination that self-help is the answer, and it is reflected in the policies of several countries. (f) Some doubts arise on the authors' comments on the use of technologies 'discarded' by the industrialized countries but which may be used profitably by Latin America. This is a complex subject, relevant to capital costs and the employment problem. Suffice it to say here that adaptation of technology to labour-intensive methods must meet criteria of economic efficiency. (g) Finally, the treatment of the employment problem in the report is far from adequate and possibly misleading. In addition to the impact of high rates of population growth on the growing labour force, there is already a volume of unemployment of some 20 to 25 per cent of the labour force. In an overall view of Latin American society, creation of employment *should be* the 'central objective of the development process', contrary to the explicit statement of the authors in Chapter 6.

Lincoln Gordon

As a member of the Steering Committee, I should like to associate myself generally with the views of Dr Aurelio Peccei and to add a few comments on the main themes of *Latin America: A Broader World Role*. The basic theses of the study, as I understand it, are : (1) that Latin America occupies an intermediate position of 'semi-development' between the large, very poor regions of Asia and Africa, on the one hand, and the highly industrialized regions of North America, Europe, and Japan on the other; and (2) that, through policies focussed on agricultural and industrial productivity, especially in manufactured products for export, reinforced by regional economic integration and organized negotiation with industrialized nations, Latin America can regain the decades lost since the Depression and achieve full participation in the kind of sustained growth and economic interdependence of equals now enjoyed by the industrialized nations.

I agree with the differentiation of Latin America from what is often and wrongly treated as a homogenous 'Third World', and with the objective of moving – in my own phrase – 'out of the Third World and into the First'. Most of Latin America has the potential to make this transition in a span of ten or twenty years, given a sympathetic and responsive attitude on the part of the presently industrialized countries. The prospects for success are greater if Latin America achieves more effective regional economic integration than if individual countries, even so large and dynamic a one as Brazil, try to act alone. It would be in the interests of the more developed countries to accelerate such a transition. That responsibility should be shared among Europe, Japan, Canada, and Australasia, as well as the United States.

Nevertheless, the historical, geographical, and institutional ties of the United States to Latin America, together with the pre-eminence of the United States in Latin America's external economic relations, continue to give her a special responsibility for leadership in that direction. In my view, the 'low profile' of United States policy towards Latin America in recent years has been carried too far. New United States initiatives are required to help bring about the wider association and ultimate integration of Latin America into the 'First World' as a whole. I agree that the economic institutions of the inter-American system should be broadened to include other industrialized nations willing to join, but the United States will continue to be 'more equal than others' in the actual workings of those restructured institutions. In short, a continuing 'special relationship' should be recognized between the United States and Latin America, but the terms of that relationship should be adjusted to the concept of incipient 'First World' status for Latin America.

In stressing the objective of integration into the 'First World', I do not imply for Latin America the goal of carbon-copy identity with growth patterns or life styles now prevalent in North America, Europe, or Japan. There is a great deal of diversity among these industrialized areas, and a growing recognition in all of them that unplanned economic growth has entailed serious environmental deterioration and other detrimental social consequences. The 'First World' concept does imply open societies with broad freedom of choice and growing equality of opportunity for their citizens. I would hope that Latin America might preserve these fundamental human values while finding its way to socio-economic patterns which avoid some of the errors of today's more industrialized nations.

On the domestic side within Latin America, I join both my colleagues, Mr Urquidi and Dr Peccei, in feeling that the study contains necessary but not sufficient prescriptions. The insufficiency lies mainly on the side of social and institutional reform and modernization. Active participation in both the process and the fruits of development is indispensable for presently marginalized urban immigrants and historically excluded rural subsistence and tenant farmers and agricultural workers. The almost singleminded focus of the study on policies for internationally competitive economic efficiency does not provide adequately for these needs.

In particular, the study underestimates the critical consequences of high rates of population growth in aggravating a whole series of social problems, including urban congestion and general underemployment and unemployment, at the same time that they divert into unproductive use a large share of the investments which might go to higher productivity. The essential question here is not the ultimate capacity of the region for accommodating a particular level of population, but the enormous drag which annual popula-

G

tion increases of 2 to 3 per cent impose on the very process of development. Certainly development will eventually bring about a reduction in birth rates, but in most of the region that process will operate far too slowly unless complemented by deliberate and organized programmes of family planning services to prevent births unwanted by parents.

There are also a number of minor points from which I would dissent, for example, portions of the historical treatment of the Alliance for Progress and certain details in the recommendations for reorganizing the Inter-American Development Bank. Neither differences of this kind nor the larger points set forth above, however, should be taken as qualifying my overall judgement that the study is a most constructive and thoughtful analysis of the dilemmas in Latin America's economic relations with the rest of the world, and that its basic thrust points in the right direction.

Aurelio Peccei

To clarify the observations I make below, a preliminary note is necessary. In my opinion, the analysis of the semi-developed condition of Latin America made in this study is not only remarkably good but also more complete than any other study that I know of. Its rationale contains many valuable departures from present thinking both in Latin America itself and in the so-called developed countries. Overall, this is a commendable effort which can provide the basis for a decisive step towards Latin Americans and their friends acquiring an adequate awareness of the difficulties that the continent will be up against in the years to come, and the new organizational forms and new policies required to meet these difficulties.

Adalbert Krieger Vasena and Javier Pazos have also made a valuable contribution to the hoped-for multilateral discussions and negotiations both among the Latin American countries and between Latin America and the industrialized countries of the northern hemisphere, at a moment when a total restructuring of the international trade and monetary systems and a radical reorganization of the world economy are needed.

While deeply appreciative of the quality of the study, I would like, by way of personal comment, to advance two warnings concerning the feasibility of the plan of action it outlines, and some observations concerning non-economic aspects which I believe, unlike what is stated or implied in the study, are essential.

My first warning concerns the capability and readiness of Latin Americans to 'organize for negotiations', which the authors declare to be indispensable. I am sure they are right. An act or acts of political will in this sense are in effect indispensable. But, I am afraid, this determination demands from the political class, supported by popular consensus and the mass media, and from industry, the unions, and the intelligentsia, even from youth and dissenters, far greater vision, mutual understanding, spirit of cooperation, pragmatism, and capacity to sacrifice details in favour

179

of general strategy, than Latin Americans have so far shown in charting their way towards continental integration.

The history of the European Community shows how difficult it is to produce any sound political philosophy and leadership, to translate them into deeds and institutions, and to reorient public opinion in order to enlarge the area of solidarity by breaking down the enclaves of national sovereignty and prejudice that are strenuously defended by petty but powerful vested interests. The result is that at this very late hour the building of a united Europe, though begun fifteen years ago, is still incomplete. With events proceeding ever faster, Latin America would need to perform the miracle of accomplishing the job in a much shorter time. This warning about the great divergence between what is needed to set Latin America on the move and what has been done so far, and therefore the gulf that exists between expectations and reality, is addressed chiefly to the three major nations, Argentina, Brazil, and Mexico, because only they, acting jointly and magnanimously, can pull Latin America together and make it participate adequately in the forthcoming round of world negotiations. If they are tempted to go it alone the whole design will probably collapse.

The second warning is of a more general character, but it should be of equal concern to Latin Americans, and everyone else. It regards the possible outcome of the momentous multilateral negotiations of 1973–74, in which the main protagonists are the United States, the enlarged European Community, and Japan. The questions on the agenda are so numerous, diverse, complex, and interrelated that they are frightening: the reorganization of the international monetary system; the role of the dollar and Special Drawing Rights, and perhaps of gold; essential questions of multinational trade, trade blocs, incentives, preferences, reciprocity, tariff and non-tariff barriers for both industrial and agricultural products; questions of government procurement and discrimination against foreign bidders, balance of payments, international investments, capital movements, fiscal policies, burden-sharing in defence; questions concerning the operation and future of the multinational enterprise; and, probably, questions of harmonization of anti-pollution standards and regulations, plus many other collateral issues, and of course the question of the overall aid needed by the less developed nations.

That these negotiations will end positively is somehow taken for granted, though there is no indication yet that the major nations are rising to the extraordinary importance of the event which should set the foundations, establish the rules, and create the instrumentalities of the world community's economic life for many years to come. In fact, not only is the agenda eminently and vitally political in a broad international sense, but it also represents the yardstick against which the industrial civilization's capacity to put the world in order and prepare for a new phase of progress will be measured. Nevertheless, the big nations seem still to consider the 1973–74 negotiations as a mammoth technical exercise, and continue to give pre-eminence to motives of domestic relevance or expediency. Therefore Latin America should both brace itself to participate intensively and effectively in those new multinational negotiations, and at the same time be ready to forge ahead substantially alone should this round conclude with partial failure or postponement.

I would parenthetically add that Latin America could usefully inject in these multilateral negotiations a sense of realism about the need for a more balanced world economy – which is in everybody's interest. It probably behoves Latin America, as the most advanced of the less developed regions, to take up a position on this issue, and show how an international reorganization and rationalization of production, based initially on the transfer of labour-intensive, low-technology industries to the developing countries, could establish a better equilibrium. This point, only touched upon in the study, should be expanded. In Europe, for example, many people do realize how much healthier it would be to decongest intensively industrialized areas and stop the socially and morally objectionable practice of 'importing' cheap labour from less developed countries, and instead move certain types of production there; but only a few so far dare to air these views openly and underscore that whatever plans even the multinational corporations may want to develop, their effectiveness can be but limited if it is not founded on a vast network of co-operative agreements among the large economic areas of the world.

The observations I am now going to make do not detract from the merits of the study. They concern the singlemindedness with which its authors have focussed their attention on matters economic, and the primordial necessity, according to them, of maximizing production, as the first and foremost step required in any process of socio-economic development. There is no doubt that a much better performance in production is necessary to improve Latin American economies and integrate them more satisfactorily in the world. But in my view, the problems of our complex modern societies, both developed and less developed, cannot be dealt with by essentially simple, linear approaches.

Latin American societies are in many ways mature, sophisticated societies, open to events that occur in the wide world, and therefore, while yearning for better life standards, they share with other peoples the ferments of this period of transition. This means that good economic management is not enough. No less effort must be devoted in most of Latin America to reaching higher levels of social justice and of education, and the activation and employment of the marginal classes – which cannot be considered just as a work force and as indirect beneficiaries of the productive process. If the collective venture of changing Latin America's condition, both internally and with respect to the rest of the world, is going to be successful, it needs intensive popular participation, and the productive effort cannot be divorced from profound social transformation. To imagine that the latter can be postponed is illusory.

Moreover, even for such a very large unit as Latin America – or the United States or Europe for that matter – production and economic development cannot be considered in isolation from the rest of the world system. Doubts are creeping in that human material growth is approaching the limits set by the availability of natural resources, and the need to preserve the global environment in our finite planet; and, as will be appreciated, a great debate is under way as to the possibility of maintaining the present growth trends of society. To ignore this in Latin America would be to make a serious mistake even if the present apprehensions will eventually be dispelled, as is to be hoped. What is questioned here is, of course, not whether Latin American economies should or should not grow, for it is beyond doubt that they must expand, and be helped to do so at a much quicker pace than those of the more developed countries. The point to be considered, if, as I believe, we are reaching the overall limits to mankind's material growth, is that this process must perforce somehow be harmonized internationally. To believe that Latin America, or any other large region of the world, can draw up independent long-term development plans, and be free to carry them out before clarifying (one way or the other) the fundamental issue of what further margins still exist for mankind's growth, would be another dangerous illusion.

Then again, this study does not attach enough importance to the factor of demographic pressure – which is higher in Latin America than anywhere in the world. Considered in isolation, some areas of Latin America, like some other parts of the world, may give the impression that it would do no harm for the population to continue increasing for still a few decades to come, and even that this growth is to be welcomed. It is, however, a mistake, in our ever more interdependent world, to imagine that privileged areas can permamently and safely subsist in isolation : for instance, areas of extremely rich people among the poor, of abundant resources among prevailing scarcity, of uncontaminated environments in the midst of pollution, or indeed sparsely inhabited zones side by side with others struggling with overcrowding. A great truth we have to learn is that the measures we may want to adopt in any country or continent facing the great problems of our time, be they those of development, or ecology, or security, or population, will, in the long run, be counterproductive if they are contrary to the measures which may be advisable for the world as a whole.

To conclude, I am sure that this study will present a challenge that will be taken up by other studies in due course, permitting on the whole a comprehensive, down-to-earth assessment of the extraordinary endeavour required to give a forward and constructive stance to the Latin American continent. And I wish to repeat that my remarks do not diminish the value of this forthright document. They are prompted by the desire to show the unprecedented complexity and magnitude of the tasks ahead, which (in Latin America and elsewhere) make new forms of co-operation imperative in our future conduct of human affairs in a world which is undergoing drastic and not yet fathomable changes within its finite dimensions.

Pierre Uri

However knowledgeable and sympathetic observers of Latin America from the industrialized world may be, their advice will always be branded as condescending and incompetent. Their task, therefore, should be rather to emphasize the changes in attitude that are required in the industrialized world so that developing countries may have a chance to accelerate their growth and improve their internal as well as external equilibrium.

The following proposals stem from the theme of this book, which is the relationship of Latin America to the industrialized world. They do not contradict, indeed they confirm, the thesis that it is high time for Latin America as a whole to steer a new course in its development and, as some of the countries have already begun to do, build up industries able to compete in export markets. That is the surest way of reducing dependence on foreign aid and financing. From this premise, a generalization springs to mind : the political precondition, without which development will still be blocked, is that the developing world should be relieved of its posture and feeling of dependence on the developed world.

First of all, bilateral dependence should disappear : that of Latin America on the United States, caused by the unwillingness of Europe and Japan to involve themselves beyond sheer profit-seeking in trade and investment. But just as obvious is the danger of too close a dependence of Africa on Europe and – although memories from the past commend caution on both sides – the rest of Asia on Japan. It would already be a great leap forward if the main powers acted jointly in giving aid to the various developing areas, creating a network of multilateral relationships in which Latin America, Africa, and Asia discovered their own identity and, by the same token, made an original contribution to world affairs.

But even this joint action, or an increase, as envisaged by the United States, in the channelling of aid through such international institutions as the World Bank, would not eliminate the asymmetry between the obligations accepted by an industrialized debtor country and the conditions imposed on the developing ones.

This point is crucial. As long as the countries of the Third World feel that they depend on discriminatory conditions of aid or investment from the industrialized world, they will blame others for their setbacks. The rivalry of nationalists from the Right and the Left will substitute a common national purpose.

It was opposition to the well-to-do that first drew the developing countries together. The Group of 77, and now of 100, which formed at the UNCTAD conferences, has led to a confrontation of indiscriminate demands and collective refusals. But this common front was composed of countries of very disparate conditions and levels of development, and it began to disintegrate in 1972 at Santiago, when several of its members realized that the advantages that were being extracted from the developed countries, especially generalized preferences, benefited some more than others and were in fact widening the gap between the most and least advanced among them.

Three major themes emerge from these observations : development without dependence, recognition of diversity in the Third World, and the search for a common interest among developed and developing countries.

These basic ideas are political, and they must be carefully followed through into application. In other words, we must try to find the means to deal with issues rather than with countries, and to create the general conditions, often in indirect ways, in which each country could discover its opportunities, and with them its responsibilities.

There is no need to review all of the problems and policies of development and to repeat what other, first-rate, minds have already expressed. The objective here is to make a few precise proposals on certain points, which would change the overall context in which development takes place and relations are established between countries at different stages of development.

The first proposal concerns the administration and financing of aid. Today, whether aid is bilateral or comes from international institutions, it goes to governments. This produces a dilemma, in that too frequently funds go to governments that one is ashamed to support, yet to withdraw them would be to deprive the people these governments tyrannize. The dilemma can be avoided only by rethinking the basic function of public aid. For the poorest countries, it serves to raise the subsistence level. Beyond that it should create hospitable conditions for investment, i.e., infrastructure and education. It is thus a transposition to a world scale of the essential ingredients of a domestic regional policy. Such a conception is all the more adapted to present circumstances as a freer flow of trade and capital brings the world increasingly together. It also shows the way to practical arrangements. Regional development banks should be set up everywhere, with special responsibility for particularly depressed zones in large countries, such as northeast Brazil, or for a region comprising a number of countries in the case of small contiguous states. Let us not delude ourselves that this new form of aid could begin without a modification of the statutes of the World Bank and other financial institutions dealing with the Third World, or without joint guarantees of the interested states. But if this proposal were adopted, at least aid and loans on favourable terms would be channelled directly into regional development, without passing through the hands of national governments.

The needed changes in the international monetary system could also be a first step towards improving the system of aid. It is surprising that international liquidity, in the form of SDRs, is created according to the allocation of quotas in the IMF, i.e., largely as a function of wealth and trade. Equity and efficiency would call for different priorities. Developed countries have normally to earn their growth in reserves. The only cases in which they benefit by a windfall are a revaluation of the price of gold or the devaluation of their own currency. Allocations in the form of gifts should be reserved for developing countries. But there is another obvious source of development finance. An increase in the price of industrial gold is profitable for countries with large reserves, but they would lose nothing *vis-à-vis* their current positions if the IMF were charged with progressively liquidating stocks of gold and transmitting profits to development institutions or otherwise earmarking profits on the sale of gold to finance aid. This would be a free resource of finance on a world scale for years to come.

These basic sources of finance are a neccessary complement to private investment, and especially direct investment, particularly by firms which, due to the size and spread of their operations, accede to a multinational status. Such investments could theoretically best achieve a rational distribution of resources, with respect both to the location of production, and the sources of allocation of funds. This distribution, however, is completely distorted by various national policies, some of which raise difficulties – expropriation, for one example – others, on the contrary, increasing their attractiveness through various facilities and tax incentives. This distortion, as well as the rivalry in the developing world, would be avoided if joint guarantee councils were set up by groups of countries, which would provide insurance against default in the case of a loan, or against expropriation without suitable indemnity in the case of direct investments. This mechanism, which would enable aid to be distributed otherwise than through the states, would also increase the negotiating capacity of developing countries *vis-à-vis* the big companies.

A complete analysis of the advantages and disadvantages of direct investments in developing countries especially those of multinational businesses, would involve a study of the contribution of capital and the cost of servicing it; of the increase in exports and savings in imports; of resources provided to or removed from states, according to the supplementary taxes they collect or the subsidies they grant; of the incentives or obstacles to the formation of domestic savings and an entrepreneurial class – the whole being mainly prospective, and being balanced by a comparison with other, purely domestic solutions. But statistics are rarely available for such an analysis of costs and benefits, which in any case would involve many problematical elements.

A scheme exists that has every possibility of maximizing the benefits and of minimizing the costs, and even more, of reducing political frictions. The large corporations of the industrialized countries have taken the initiative in implementing it, first in Latin America under the name Adela, followed by PICA in Asia and an organization now being formed in Africa. These groups are constituted via the subscriptions of large firms from the various countries, with no one of them having a predominant position. Thus, they are genuinely multinational. They form associations with local partners, who participate in the management. After a period of development, all the interests are turned over to the local partner. In this way, local savings and management potential are encouraged rather than stifled. The financial capabilities of the participating corporations allow for loans and credit in addition to direct capital. As money becomes available, it can be reinvested in new projects, so that the impact of development is more widely diffused and the burden on the balance of payments caused by debt servicing or profit remittances is as limited as possible. If all the developing continents adopted this scheme, there would be a basis of agreement that would eliminate a great number of risks and conflicts.

It is imperative that development should not be hindered by sudden losses of income from exports. Many developing nations are exporters of primary products. Contrary to what has long been believed, there is no long-term trend disfavouring these products and favouring industrial products of which these same nations are buyers. In fact, the last decade has in general proved favourable for primary commodities, except for agricultural products, which are in any case exported mostly by the industrialized nations. And increasing demand, along with the exhaustion of resources, can only tend to raise prices. On the other hand, the fluctuations are violent. For food products, they are due primarily to variation of supply, for example an abundant coffee or cacao harvest. For primary industrial products, price tendencies are a function of the industrial growth rate of the developed countries. Indeed, industrial activity being constant, substitution and technical economies of utilization will reduce demand. This reduction should be compensated for by increased industrial production. A further increase is then necessary to absorb the growth of production of primary goods.

Thus, the trend of primary products reveals not only the situation of the producers but also the risk of inflation, or on the contrary of deflation, in the industrialized countries themselves. In other words, it is the prime indicator of the world monetary situation. From this, one should infer an essential element for the reform of the international monetary system : the creation of SDRs might be accelerated or decelerated as a function of the trend of primary products. This would also provide for compensatory financing, in as much as the export losses of each country are attributable to the weakness of the international market for its products. Such a mechanism would serve as a stabilizer on a global scale, giving primary producers the means to sustain their demand for industrial goods and industry in turn to maintain the demand for primary products, which would uphold their prices.

Not all developing nations have an important base of exportable natural resources at their disposal and, anyway, with increasing productivity, employment cannot be guaranteed on this sole foundation. Thus it is imperative that industry develop and that it find new outlets. What has been demanded by the Third World, partially accepted by the European Community and Japan, and not ratified by the United States, is generalized preferences. Within certain quantitative limits and with the exception of some sensitive products, the European Communiy has abolished duties on manufactured goods from developing countries. But no sooner is the system implemented than it proves disappointing. The most advanced of the developing countries fill all of the available quotas, further reducing the access of the least developed nations to the international market. Moreover, preferences are granted at the expense of other exporters; they offer no guarantees to developing nations that they can compete with the internal producers on the national markets they seek to penetrate.

A totally different scheme would solve the initial difficulties of new industrial exports and gradually transfer the advantages from the countries in a position to benefit from them initially to others at various stages of development. These countries should, in one way or another, be allowed to apply to their new exports a rate of exchange different from that prevailing for their traditional exports. One practical way would involve the choice of an inter-mediate rate of exchange, the imposition of a tax on traditional exports, and a use of the proceeds of such a tax to subsidize the new exports. It is immediately clear that the rate of subsidization per unit of merchandise would tend to zero while exports of new products grew in comparison with exports of traditional products. In other words, the dual exchange rate would be only temporary and a single rate would gradually re-emerge as the device proved effective. However, other less developed nations would in their turn benefit from these new opportunities for export and development.

Such mechanisms will still not allow for the development of industries where they are most economical, if developed countries continue to respond through increased restrictions on imports which compete with their internal production. They have no right to accuse developing nations of pushing import substitution too far if they condemn them to do so through their own tariff structures, which impede the processing of natural resources where they originate. This is evident in industrialized nations which receive primary products without duties but impose a duty on semi-refined products. These duties may, at first glance, seem minimal; compared with the margin of transformation, that is, the added value, they are, on the contrary, prohibitive. Two examples come to mind: refined copper versus ore and soluble versus green coffee. Quantitative restrictions of all kinds and customs duties varying with the stage of processing converge under the notion of effective protection as distinct from nominal protection. This effective pro-tection is the greater, the larger the gap between duties applicable to outputs and inputs. It is all the greater if restrictions of one sort or another, or preferences in public procurement, make in-ternal prices higher than international prices. In other words, effective protection is measured by the excess value added in the internal price over the would-be price under free competition. We shall not go here into the various corrections that should be introduced in order to take monopoly effects into account, nor the modifications of exchange rates that would become necessary if effective protection were reduced. The principle should be adopted in the forthcoming international negotiations to put a ceiling on effective protection and then to reduce it.

In the developed countries, effective protection is especially great in industries employing unskilled labour. An end to this distortion and the establishment of a rational international division of labour will come about only if the industrialized nations decide to give the needed breadth to methods of conversion. Labour must be protected from the risks of the changes without which there is no progress. Better still, any change of employment ought to become a chance for promotion. An analysis of the disparities in wages among economic sectors and firms reveals the advantage to labour of such a progressive conversion, of abandoning underpaid jobs and transferring to more productive economic activities at normal salaries. Such a policy, if pursued with the necessary vigour and continuity, would raise the standard of living in the industrialized nations themselves as much as they would allow its improvement in the developing countries.

The developing nations can grasp this opportunity for export-oriented industrialization only if they are also assured of a market extending beyond their national boundaries, and with more than their own feeble purchasing power. For them, regional integration is even more necessary than for the nations of an advanced continent such as Europe. Appropriate means still remain to be found for countries constantly threatened by balance-of-payments difficulties. The inequalities in size and in stages of development of countries within the same continent must also be taken into account. For political at least as much as for economic reasons, sub-regional groupings may be a prerequisite for small nations, in order to establish a substantial initial market, create new industries, and approach equality with larger or more populous neighbouring states.[1]

Beyond this, still another idea is worth consideration. It would not demand the same firm commitments to reduce trade barriers that the Europeans could agree to, knowing that the diversity and dynamism of their exports would furnish them with the means to pay for freer imports. Developing nations, as parties to an agreement, would undertake to increase the share of their imports from each other each time they achieved an increase in their over-all exports. The impact and the double consequence of such a policy are obvious. It rests on a genuine possibility of increasing purchases, and it is flexible enough to allow, when necessary, the import of needed equipment goods from the most advanced producers. A primary effect would be to provoke a chain reaction. If A buys more from B, B can in turn buy more from A or from C, and so on. At first, each country would opt for what it most sorely lacks; but soon a process of integration of production itself would get under way. There would also be another crucial effect. For one or more industrialized countries to allow imports under generalized preferences would have but a pinpoint effect on the developing nation which reaps the benefit. This scheme, however, would spread the advantage among a greater number of countries. Thus, as with the conditions that will make a new international division of labour acceptable, the common interest of the developed and developing worlds might be substituted for their confrontation.

Are these utopian projects or un-negotiable reforms? When the European Common Market began to be planned, it was considered utopian. Two years later, when the project was ready, public opinion was ripe. It is essential to start on time, which means long in advance. These proposals may appear bold; they will be elaborated and justified in a separate book, *Development without Dependence.*

NOTE

[1] The proposition that sub-regional groups may well be the most effective first step towards region-wide integration is also supported by John Tuthill.

Geoffrey Wallinger

My immediate reaction on laying down the final draft of *Latin America: A Broader World Role*, might be colloquially summarized in the words: 'Excellent, hard-hitting stuff, that will certainly shock much "establishment thinking" – in Latin America and in the rest of the world!' And I at once recalled that, at an early meeting of the Atlantic Institute's Steering Committee for this project, we were all agreed that what was needed of our authors was a work that would excite discussion; this must not, we said, be just another evocative survey of the relationships of the region with the more industrialized countries of the northern hemisphere, but rather a challenge to argument about what the structure of those relationships should be in the future. This book poses that challenge in able, original, and forceful terms.

Lest, however, it be thought that I am suggesting that provocation for provocation's sake is an adequate reason for writing a book, let me at once add that, whatever doubts and queries the authors have provoked in my rather 'establishment'-trained mind, my tribute is deeply sincere both as to the cogency and coherence of their analysis – by its very nature a contentious matter – and as to the forthright clarity of their advocacy of policies for the future – a no less contentious subject!

This said, may I venture two comments? The first concerns the political feasibility, in any foreseeable future, of the acceptance by the governments of Latin America of the concept of 'integrated organization for negotiation on a region-wide basis', which is an essential element in the policies the writers advocate. The achievement of a high degree of such integration is eminently desirable and it is therefore perfectly appropriate that the desirability be stated. It is, moreover, significant that it should have been stated, in forceful and urgent language, by two eminent Latin Americans of differing backgrounds, of nationality, ideology, and experience. But I trust that they will forgive me if I say that I find myself wondering whether this meeting of minds at what is an optimum

intellectual level may be thought to disclose the difficulty of finding areas of agreement at those earthier levels of practical politics
at which decisions are made, especially at a time when nationalistic
and protectionist fervours seem to have all too positive an influence
on political leaderships – and not only in Latin America.

My second comment flows from the first; for it seems to me that
the book dwells perhaps too heavily upon political decisions and
inter-governmental relations, and pays too little attention to the
role of the private sector. It is true that a framework of political
decisions and formal legislation is needed for private enterprise to
operate, and the authors state very lucidly what is needed in this
respect; they might have been rather more explicit on the responsibilities of the private sector for giving concrete expression to
official policy.

Let me give an example. One of the main arguments put forward by the authors is that Latin America's development depends
to a great extent on more efficient and larger-scale production, in
both agriculture and industry; only by better productive organization can Latin American farmers and industrialists reduce their
costs and prices and, by implication, widen their markets. The
economic policies needed for these aims to be achieved, the authors
point out, are the responsibility of governments. No one can
question the truth of this assertion; but the argument could perhaps be balanced with a parallel and specific emphasis on the need
for more energetic and effective marketing by private enterprise,
with all that this implies in terms of quality control, punctuality
and volume of delivery, and ancillary services. The dangers inherent in an overproduction of unmarketable goods require no
definition, efficient large-scale production is rightly stressed as one
of the keys to Latin America's economic growth; but what perhaps
needs to be explicitly stated is that the productive potential should
be expanded and modernized in step with the penetration of
markets.

The pressing need for Latin America to increase its share of
world exports is fully recognized in Chapter 11, and the authors
very correctly recognize the need for a co-ordinated regional trade
strategy. They welcome the achievements of the UNCTAD, and
the cautious adoption by the industrialized countries of generalized
preferences. Negotiations at government level are a necessary
foundation for the expansion of exports; but the argument could
again be taken a step further by suggesting that, when it comes to
real business, it is the private sector entrepreneurs who have to do
a scientifically planned job of marketing. In a world in which the
expansion of trade has to be achieved in the teeth of protectionism,

one of the primary tasks of the Latin Americans is to make the rest of the world aware of the region's productive potential and at the same time to identify the nature and extent of world demand, even to the extent of detailed product analysis. Governments can help or hinder this kind of activity; but little will be achieved unless an informed and energetic private sector is determined on success.

There would perhaps be advantage in such efforts being conducted on a co-ordinated regional basis, and ideas of this kind have been promoted with some success by the Centro Interamericano para la Promoción de las Exportaciones (CIPE); but actual sales and shipments are in the end better conducted by individual firms and agents, the past record of state trading organizations not being strikingly good.

The authors foresee for the CECLA an important role in promoting Latin American integration, in co-ordinating the region's negotiations with the rest of the world, and in contributing Latin American views in world trade and monetary discussions. The Inter-American Development Bank is also seen as an important agent in Latin America's financial relations with the rest of the world, and in managing the Latin American Integration Fund and Industrialization Fund (both admirable suggestions). Could not a vastly enlarged role, suitably financed, be imagined for the CIPE, in the important area of marketing?

The breadth and depth of the issues that this admirably forthright book seeks to cover tend, in themselves, to make any critique seem a little captious. But as I offer the above comments, I am sure that both Dr Krieger Vasena and Sr Javier Pazos will know that I am, above all, grateful to have this opportunity publicly to express to them my humble and sincere congratulations on a remarkable achievement.

Glossary of Regional and International Organizations in which Latin American Countries Participate[1]

Adela Investment Company S.A., was founded in 1964 by a group of prominent private industrial and financial enterprises. In 1972 the company had 242 shareholders, all of them well-known companies from Europe, the United States, Canada, Japan, and Latin America. It is the purpose of Adela to foster socio-economic progress in Latin America by stimulating private enterprise through providing development services, technology, and financing, including equity as a minority investor, to viable new projects and for the expansion of existing enterprises. In the first eight years of its existence, Adela under its long-term investment disbursed $104 million to 124 companies in 21 Latin American countries, either for new projects or for the expansion of existing companies. Adelatec, the company's subsidiary active in business development, management, and technical services, undertakes assignments throughout Latin America, partly for Adela itself but mostly for third parties. A relatively recent addition to Adela's service activities is the development of trade, mostly in finished and semi-finished products, both within the area and to the world markets. Head Office : Lima, Peru.

Andean Development Corporation (Corporación Andina de Fomento – CAF): a development bank set up in 1969 by the Cartagena Agreement (see below) specifically to finance the economic expansion of the Andean Group countries. The participating members are Bolivia, Chile, Colombia, Ecuador, Peru, and Venezuela; this last country was a founder member of the CAF although it did not join the Andean Group until 1973. The head office of the Corporation is in Caracas, Venezuela.

Andean Group (Grupo Andino), sometimes also referred to as the Cartagena Agreement, was set up in 1969 by Bolivia, Chile,

Colombia, Ecuador, and Peru, who were joined in 1973 by Venezuela. This Andean sub-regional agreement was approved by the LAFTA Executive Committee. It aims to assist the development of member countries through economic integration, to establish favourable conditions for the development of the LAFTA common market, to eliminate internal tariff barriers, to introduce a common external tariff by 1980, and to establish within the Group common rulings governing the activities of foreign investors. The administrative Junta has its offices in Lima, Peru.

Caribbean Development Bank was established in January 1970, with an equity capital of $50 million, to stimulate economic growth and development in the region by assisting members in the co-ordination of their development programmes, by mobilizing additional financial resources from within and outside the region, by providing technical assistance, and by promoting public and private investment in development projects. Its membership comprises the CARIFTA member countries, the Bahamas, the British Virgin Islands, the Cayman Islands and the Turks and Caicos Islands, and since 1970, Colombia. Regional governments hold 60 per cent of the Bank's capital, and the remaining 40 per cent is provided by other governments (Britain and Canada).

Caribbean Free Trade Association (*CARIFTA*) was founded in January 1967 by Antigua, Barbados, and Guyana; membership has since expanded with the admission of Grenada, Jamaica, Montserrat, St Christopher-Nevis-Anguilla, St Lucia, St Vincent, and Trinidad and Tobago. To achieve its goals of promoting trade expansion and diversification within the area, and encouraging the economic development of members, provision was made for the immediate removal of all tariffs on trade among members (with the exception of certain manufactured goods), and for incentives to establish industry and develop agriculture.

CECLA, see *Special Committee for Latin American Co-ordination.*

CECON, see *Special Committee for Consultation and Negotiation.*

Central American Bank for Economic Integration was founded in May 1961 by El Salvador, Guatemala, Honduras, and Nicaragua (later joined by Costa Rica) to promote economic integration among its members and a balanced economic development between the countries; to finance projects which will further these aims and to develop trade in the CACM.

Central American Common Market (*CACM*) was established in 1960 by the Treaty of Managua, and comprises Costa Rica, Guatemala, El Salvador, Honduras, and Nicaragua. Its objectives include the elimination of all tariffs and trade barriers between members, and the establishment of a common external tariff for the rest of the world.

CIAP, see *Inter-American Committee on the Alliance for Progress*.

CIES, see *Inter-American Economic and Social Council*.

Economic Commission for Latin America, United Nations (ECLA) was established in 1948 by the United Nations Economic and Social Council as one of the four Regional Economic Commissions. Its efforts are concentrated on development policy; the Secretariat undertakes theoretical analyses of economic problems and formulates policy proposals for economic development. It is also concerned with foreign trade and external financing, integration, employment and population problems, policies for reducing regional imbalances among ECLA countries, and science and technology, mainly the transfer of expertise and the assimilation of techniques.

Group of Twenty (Committee of the IMF Board of Governors on Reform of the International Monetary System and Related Issues) was set up in June 1972 by the Board of Governors of the International Monetary Fund to be a representative committee of both developed and developing countries which would 'provide a forum in which momentum can be maintained at a high policy-making level for all aspects of reform of the international monetary system'. It is to give full attention to the interrelation between these matters and existing or prospective arrangements among countries – including those involving international trade, the flow of capital investment, or development assistance – which could affect the attainment of the purposes of the Fund under the present or amended articles.

Inter-American Committee on the Alliance for Progress (Comité Interamericano de la Alianza para el Progresso, CIAP) was set up in November 1963 to act as the permanent Executive Committee of the Inter-American Economic and Social Council, and the multilateral representative of the Alliance for Progress. It co-ordinates Alliance action, and in particular evaluates the internal development efforts of each member country in order to determine the needs and availabilities of external financing; it also promotes co-ordination of development assistance among lending agencies.

Inter-American Development Bank (IDB) was established in 1959 with the purpose of contributing to the process of economic development in Latin America. The Bank receives its funds from subscriptions of its member countries, from loans obtained on international capital markets, and from transfers from individual countries administered as special funds. The Latin American members[2] have contributed substantially to financing projects, though the greater part of the Bank's resources are supplied by the United States or raised on the United States capital markets. The Bank's funds are broken down into ordinary capital lent at rates close to those prevailing in the commercial market, and Funds for Special Operations that bear a concessional interest rate, most of which have been supplied by the United States. In the first decade of its existence, the IDB contributed one-third of all the official financing received by the region. Head Office : Washington, D.C.

Inter-American Economic and Social Council (Consejo Interamericano Económico y Social, CIES) was created in 1945 to supersede the Inter-American Financial and Economic Advisory Committee. It was incorporated in the Charter of the OAS in 1948. Meetings at ministerial level are held annually to review the Alliance for Progress, based on the prior review of the CIAP (the permanent executive committee of CIES). It also acts as the co-ordinating agency of inter-American activities in the economic and social fields. The General Secretariat of the OAS acts as the Secretariat of CIES.

Latin American Free Trade Association (LAFTA) was established in June 1961 on the ratification of the Montevideo Treaty signed in February 1960, and now numbers 11 members : Argentina, Bolivia, Brazil, Chile, Colombia, Ecuador, Mexico, Paraguay, Peru, Uruguay, and Venezuela. It aims gradually to eliminate from the reciprocal trade of its members all types of duties and restrictions that affect the importation of goods from any of the others. The Permanent Executive Committee is empowered to set up consultative commissions and to call on other bodies for technical assistance. Secretariat : Montevideo, Uruguay.

Organization of American States (OAS) was established in 1948 as the successor to the Pan American Union, which had been founded in 1890. Its objectives are to prevent possible causes of difficulties and ensure pacific settlement of any disputes among member states; to provide for common action in the case of aggression (under the Inter-American Treaty of Reciprocal Assistance signed in 1947); to seek solutions to any political, juridical, or economic problems; and to promote, through co-operative action, economic, social, and cultural development. The Council of the OAS is composed of one representative of each of the 23 members[3]. The Council's three organs (each comprising representatives of all members) are the Inter-American Economic and Social Council, the Inter-American Cultural Council, and the

Pan American Union. Headquarters : Washington, D.C.

Organization of Petroleum Exporting Countries (OPEC) was established in September 1960 by Iran, Iraq, Kuwait, Saudi Arabia, and Venezuela to form a more united front in preventing the unilateral reduction of prices by international oil companies. Indonesia, Libya, Qatar, Algeria, and others have since joined. The members account for over 50 per cent of world oil production, and 85 per cent of oil exports. The 1971 rise in the price of crude oil by 35 cents a barrel, from the average posted price of Persian Gulf oil of $1.80, demonstrated the members' capacity for concerting action effectively. OPEC is also endeavouring to make common production arrangements, to improve the application of profit-sharing clauses, and to codify oil legislation. Venezuela has been especially active in attempting to harmonize production growth rates among members. Headquarters : Vienna.

Special Committee for Consultation and Negotiation (Comité Especial para Consulta y Negociación, CECON) was created in February 1970 in response to the Consensus of Viña del Mar, drawn up by CECLA. It is a permanent instrument for consultation and negotiation between Latin America, acting as one bargaining unit, and the United States, and it seeks to eliminate tariff and non-tariff restrictions in the United States market, to reduce freight costs and improve communications, and to accelerate and further the development of tourism in Latin America.

Special Committee for Latin American Co-ordination (Comité Especial de Coordinación Latino Americana, CECLA) was created in November 1963 to act as a co-ordinating organ, among the Latin American members of the OAS, on matters relating to the first meeting of UNCTAD. Provision was made for the United States to participate as an observer. CECLA's role as a political organ was stressed, though that role was limited to information and co-ordination. Secretarial facilities were provided by the Secretariat of the CIES. Originally CECLA's work was to end with the filing of its report to the member governments a few days before the inauguration of UNCTAD, but it was subsequently decided to maintain CECLA as an informal co-ordinating body, chiefly on trade matters.

United Nations Conference on Trade and Development (UNCTAD) was set up in December 1964 as a permanent organ of the United Nations General Assembly, with a membership comprising all countries that are members of the United Nations or any of its agencies. Its objectives include the improvement of international commercial and financial relations, especially between the developed and the developing nations. Its meetings have not only given opportunities for confrontations between rich and poor regions and countries but have achieved tangible improvements in their relations. There have been three plenary meetings since it was founded, in Geneva, New Delhi, and Santiago, Chile. The Trade and Development Board meets twice yearly, the UNCTAD-GATT Trade Centre is a permanent body functioning alongside the UNCTAD Secretariat in Geneva. The conference meets about once every three years; between sessions the 55-member Trade and Development Board meets twice a year to ensure the continuity of its work.

NOTES

[1] This is not a complete list; it is intended to provide brief descriptions of some of the organizations mentioned in the book.

[2] Argentina, Barbados, Bolivia, Brazil, Chile, Colombia, Costa Rica, Dominican Republic, Ecuador, El Salvador, Guatemala, Haiti, Honduras, Mexico, Nicaragua, Panama, Paraguay, Peru, Trinidad and Tobago, Uruguay, Venezuela.

[3] Argentina, Barbados, Bolivia, Brazil, Chile, Colombia, Costa Rica, Dominican Republic, Ecuador, El Salvador, Guatemala, Haiti, Honduras, Jamaica, Mexico, Nicaragua, Panama, Paraguay, Peru, Trinidad and Tobago, United States, Uruguay, Venezuela.

Index

Printed in Great Britain by
Tonbridge Printers Limited
Peach Hall Works, Tonbridge, Kent